The Essential Book of
SHELLFISH

ROBERT H. ROBINSON

By Robert H. Robinson

First printing: February, 1983
Second printing: August, 1983

©Robert H. Robinson, 1983
LIBERTY PUBLISHING COMPANY
Cockeysville, Maryland

Published by:

Liberty Publishing Company, Inc.
50 Scott Adam Road
Cockeysville, Maryland 21030

Library of Congress #82-84274
ISBN 0-89709-040-3

Manufactured USA

To my wife, my inspiration,
who once believed the easiest way
to get food from shellfish would be
to have someone else do it.

This delightful book is the most complete,
practical guide available today

Table of Contents

Introduction

More blood has probably been shed opening clams and oysters than during a small war. At one well-attended oyster-eat (the kind that sports a local band and sawdust on the floor), there may be two dozen accidental stabbings, as compared to one intentional. However, by following the illustrations and instructions in this book, you should be able to open the most obstinate shellfish and remain completely unscathed.

Besides freeing you of worry about whether you've had your tetanus booster shot, this guide shows you how to get every bit of food from shellfish. Waitresses report horror stories of customers who miss eating tails of Maine lobsters or the claws of blue crabs. Seafood has become too much a luxury for such waste. Nothing should be lost. But to accomplish this goal, the opening of shellfish has to become a craft. And the greatest challenge is the blue crab.

Those of us who buy crab meat at the store, cook it and then spend some time removing bits of shell, realize that the craft of dismantling a blue crab is known by few people.

Additional information on specific topics in this book may be found in individual volumes of my *Shellfish Series*. The titles and the address for ordering can be found on page 153.

R. H. Robinson

Cleaning

Before clams are opened they should be cleaned by scrubbing the shells with a stiff brush under running water.

Often clams contain sand. They will discharge this and other foreign matter if placed in a pail of sea water or a mixture of one gallon fresh water with one-third cup salt. Leave for several hours. You may want to change the water several times.

Another way to insure the clams are free from grit is, after opening them into a bowl with their juice, to remove each clam and wash it under running water, working the clam with your thumb and forefinger. Place clams in a separate bowl, then pour clam juice into a tall clear glass. Of course, leave what dregs have already settled in the bowl. After more matter has settled in the glass, top off the juice into another clear glass or pour back with the washed clams.

You can also strain clam juice through cheese cloth.

Keeping Fresh

Clams live longer out of the water than they do in still, unaerated water in a pot, for they need oxygen. As with any shellfish, keep them in a cool dark place, such as the vegetable bin in your refrigerator. Fresh clams can keep for weeks, although the longer they are kept, the stronger the taste. If they are slow in closing their shells when you handle them, you should plan a meal with them soon or freeze them. If they don't close at all, throw them out. Bivalves "tell" when they are unsafe to eat—if they don't close when raw and if they don't open when cooked.

Freezing

Clams come prepackaged for freezing. Simply put whole clams which have been rinsed in a plastic bag in the freezer. Clams can also be opened and the meat and juice placed in containers and frozen.

Sizes

The larger the shrimp, oyster, crab and lobster the more it costs. However, the smaller the clam, the more it costs.

Here's a gauge for determining the designation of a clam by its size.

Littlenecks	Max. Width	2¼ inches
Cherrystones or Steamers	Max. Width	3 inches
Chowders		Above 3 inches

For some reason, the most difficult (and the most hazardous) way of opening a hard clam is the one most often used. This method is holding the clam with its hinge against the palm of your hand and then, usually with a grimace on your face, trying to force a sharp bladed knife between the shells in the front.

One easier way is shown in the following illustrations. Note that the blade of the knife shown in the first drawing is thin, narrow and has a sharp point. A child could bend it out of shape. Knives, other than this vegetable knife, that can be used are fish fillet knives, pen knives or even oyster knives.

In the back of the clam near the hinge is a ligament which looks like a protruding black lip. Moving toward the front, where the ligament ends, is a weak spot.

Insert the blade at this weak spot. It should slide in easily.

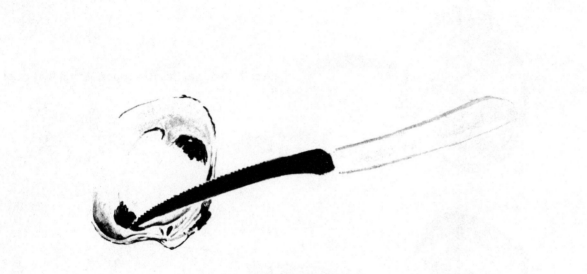

Inside the clams are two muscles—shown by the dark areas on the drawing—which hold the clam shut.

Sever these muscles with the knife, using a pumping movement.

Now that the clam is part way opened, insert knife blade in the front of the clam and scrape meat free from top and bottom shells. The muscles are too tough to eat so leave in. With larger clams you may want to use a larger bladed knife to cut out meat.

Another way to open a clam is to cut away edge of the shell to provide an opening for a knife. A file as shown in illustration is not really necessary. You can scrape the edge of the clam on cement or crack the edge with any hard object, even the back of a spoon. The object is to provide an opening for the knife blade. One good point to this technique is that the clam meat is left whole and isn't cut in half as in the other methods. You can file the opening on either side or edge of the bivalve.

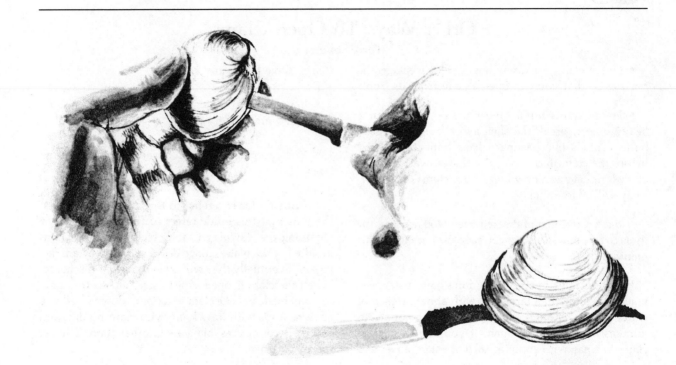

Insert blade and cut muscles.

Then go in front and cut out body.

Other Ways To Open Clams
(For Cooking)

• Freeze clams for a few hours. This weakens the muscles so that you can open a clam from its front.

• Freeze clams for a longer period, then with a heavy object, break the shell away from the frozen body. This is like peeling a hard boiled egg. Next before the clam meat and juice thaws, wash off bits of shell under running water. Place clams in a bowl. They will thaw quickly.

• Bake clams in a preheated oven (450 degrees) for three to five minutes. You can save the juice using this method.

• Steam clams open. If you don't have a steamer, place a colander in a large pan with about an inch of water or just enough to keep steam for about ten minutes or until clams open. If you like, just place clams in a pan with about an inch of water, cover and steam. Save broth and strain.

• Place clams in a microwave oven for two minutes. You can watch them open.

• You can place clams on barbecue grill and cook open.

• With all due reverence to the late Euell Gibbons, the writer of this guide refers to this method as the "Stalking the Yawning Clam," technique: Put clams in salted or sea water, hinge down so that they are facing up. Eventually they will open to feed or discharge. When the clam is open as if to say "ah" as to a doctor, slip blade in. The clam will clamp down so all you have to do is withdraw knife with clam holding on. Cut the two muscles and stalk another clam. This requires patience.

Cocktail Sauce

Chilled fresh clams on the half shell need little more than a few drops of lemon juice. However, if you would like a cocktail sauce, here's one you can probably make at the table of any seafood restaurant.

¼ cup catsup
1 teaspoon Worcestershire sauce
1 teaspoon lemon
½ teaspoon horseradish

Mix together. If possible let stand for an hour or so. Also provide a jar of horseradish in case some people like it hot.

Clam and Avocado Soup

Clam juice
Sherry Wine
Avocado (sliced)
Lemon or lime (sliced)

If you have an excess of clam juice, clean it by pouring it through cheese cloth. Add to this clam juice an equal amount of sherry wine. (You may wish to make this soup even when no fresh clam juice is available; in that case, substitute bottled clam juice; the amount you use depends on how many servings of soup you wish to prepare).Simmer this mixture in a saucepan for five minutes. Pour broth over slices of avocado. Add thin slices of lemon or lime. This soup can be served either hot or cold.

Two Quick and Easy Clam Chowders

Some people prefer that their clam chowders "age" for at least 24 hours. Here are two recipes for chowders which you can tell your guests have been aged properly. More than likely they will believe you even though the chowder was made only ten minutes before.

These are excellent recipes because they combine the broken down characteristics of aged vegetables with the freshness of clams.

Clams in the chowder recipes should be chopped, ground or shredded. The quickest way is to place clams and juice in a blender and blend.

Another way is to place clams on a metal sheet or plate and place in freezer until clams are almost frozen, which takes only a few minutes. You can then chop the clams as you do celery.

Instant Clam Chowder (I)

(New England Style)

1 slice bacon cooked and sliced in small pieces
1 can cream of celery soup
½ can milk
½ can water or chicken broth

1 cup or more of clams with juice
¾ teaspoon Old Bay seasoning (preferably) or any other seafood seasoning
    Mix, heat and serve. Serves 4.

Instant Clam Chowder (II)

(Manhattan Style)

1 slice bacon cooked and sliced in small pieces
1 can of vegetable vegetarian soup or
  Minestrone soup
1 can of V-8, Clamato or Tomato Juice
2 cups or more of clams and juice

1 teaspoon thyme
1 teaspoon chopped parsley

Mix and simmer for five minutes. Serves 4.

Clam Chowder the Hard Way

If you want to make clam chowder from scratch, here's a simple recipe.

¼ cup sliced bacon strips
½ cup chopped onion
2 cups chopped celery
2 cups clams and juice
1 cup diced potatoes
2 cups of milk or 2 cups chicken broth

Fry bacon until brown.

Add onions and celery to bacon and sautee until tender.

Add clams, juice and potatoes and cook until potatoes are done.

Add milk or broth and heat just to boiling point. Serves 4.

Clam Tempura

Tempura can be used for cooking almost any shellfish and most vegetables.

1 cup flour
1 cup iced water
1 egg barely beaten

Mix together flour and iced water.

Note: for a crisper batter add ½ cup iced water and ½ cup cornstarch. (You may substitute pancake mix for flour.)

Dip clams (or other shellfish) into beaten egg, then the batter, and then cook in hot oil, preferably peanut oil because it does not spatter.

Lemon Tempura Batter

1 cup flour
½ cup lemon juice
½ cup beer

Mix ingredients.

Open clams, drain, pat dry, dip into batter and fry in hot peanut oil.

Salt and pepper to taste.

Stuffed Clams

This dish can be called stuffed clams or deviled clams. Cherry stones or littlenecks are not really necessary; simply blend clams in blender or grind them in a meat grinder or chop them.

Save shells after opening clams.

The combinations for this dish are unlimited and the amounts given are simply suggestive.

1 cup minced clams with juice
1 cup of cubed bread or shredded bread
1 teaspoon minced green pepper
1 teaspoon minced onion

1 teaspoon chopped celery
¼ teaspoon Worcestershire sauce
a few drops of tabasco sauce
Grated Parmesan cheese
Bacon strips
Paprika

Mix clams and bread. Add pepper, onion, celery, Worcestershire and Tabasco (optional). Spoon into shells and sprinkle cheese, then place bacon slices on top. Bake in oven at 350° for 10 minutes. Add dashes of paprika and broil until bacon is crisp.

Clams Casino

Use same recipe as above, but use whole clams and omit the bread.

Clam Bake *Sans* Sand

To have an old fashioned clambake on a public beach today, you would probably have to have permits from several government agencies including the Army Corps of Engineers. Anyway, the New England clambakes that call for seaweed and rocks are impractical in many areas. There aren't many rocks, and the proper kind of seaweed—rockweed—is not that plentiful.

Here's a recipe called Clambake *Sans* Sand for the home stove or barbecue grill. The amounts of ingredients are flexible.

Traditionally, the corn on the cob is cooked along with the shellfish and the other vegetables. But it's suggested that the corn be cooked separately because it takes up so much room in the pot and it neither adds to nor absorbs enough of the taste of clams to warrant inclusion.

This meal is well worth cooking, if just for the base for the clam broth.

This is for a very hungry four.

Water

Enough large clams to cover the bottom of the pot.

Lettuce, spinach, corn husks, or any other greens— enough to make three layers in pot. (Approximately 2 heads of lettuce.)

4 peeled onions and 4 unpeeled potatoes—either white or sweet

1 chicken cut up (salted and peppered)

1 dozen cherry stone clams or steamers, mussels, lobsters, lobster tails, crabs, any shellfish and fillets of fish.

Put about 1 inch of water in the bottom of a large pot. Add clams and bring water to a boil, then lower to a simmer. Place a layer of greens over the clams. Place potatoes and onions on top of the greens. Cover with another layer of greens. Place chicken on this layer of greens, then cover with a third layer. Cover pot tightly and steam for 45 minutes. Add the remaining seafood, re-cover pot, and let steam for 20 minutes or until shellfish is done and clams have opened.

For ease in lifting out the layers of food, cheesecloth can be used to hold foods together in packets.

Clam Broth

1 quart broth from clambake
1 cup butter
¼ cup flour
2 teaspoons English mustard
2 teaspoons ground black pepper

Pour broth into a saucepan, add butter, flour, mustard and pepper. Stir until boiling. Dip clams into broth or serve as soup.

Clams in Shells

2 cans (6½ or 7 ounces each) canned clams, minced
or chopped
12 ounces shell macaroni
2 or 3 garlic cloves, minced
½ cup grated parmesan cheese
⅓ cup chopped parsley
¼ cup melted margarine or butter
½ teaspoon salt
⅛ teaspoon pepper

Drain clams and reserve liquid. Cook macaroni according to package directions.

Meanwhile, in a 2-quart saucepan, cook clam liquid with garlic over low heat until reduced to one half. Drain macaroni well. Combine macaroni, clams and liquid, cheese, parsley, margarine, salt, and pepper. Heat. If desired, portion the mixture into six 8-ounce individual baking shells or ramekins. Garnish with additional Parmesan cheese and broil for 2 to 3 minutes until lightly browned.

Makes 6 entree servings or 12 appetizer servings.

Steamed Clams in Wine Broth

3 pounds littleneck or razor clams in the shell

½ cup dry white wine

2 tablespoons margarine or butter

½ cup melted margarine or butter

1 lemon or lime, cut into wedges

Wash clam shells thoroughly with a brush under cold running water. Using a large pot with a rack or a steamer, place wine and 2 tablespoons margarine in bottom of pot. Place rack in pot. Arrange clams on the rack. Cover. Steam for 6 to 10 minutes or until clams open. Arrange clams in their shells in shallow soup bowls and pour steaming broth over clams. Serve with melted margarine and lemon wedges.

Makes 6 appetizer servings.

Pilgrims Clam Pie

3 dozen shell clams
or
3 cans (8 ounces each) minced clams
1½ cups water
¼ cup margarine or butter
½ cup sliced fresh mushrooms
2 tablespoons minced onion
¼ cup all-purpose flour
⅛ teaspoon liquid hot pepper sauce
¼ teaspoon dry mustard
¼ teaspoon salt
⅛ teaspoon white pepper
1 cup reserved clam liquor
1 cup half and half
1 tablespoon lemon juice
2 tablespoons chopped parsley
2 tablespoons chopped pimiento
Pastry for a 1-crust 9 inch pie
1 egg, beaten

Wash clam shells thoroughly. Place clams in a large pot with water. Bring to a boil and simmer for 8 to 10 minutes or until clams open. Remove clams from shell and cut into fourths. Reserve 1 cup clam liquor. (OR: If using canned clams, drain and reserve 1 cup liquor). In a skillet melt margarine. Add mushrooms and onion and cook until tender. Stir in flour, mustard, liquid hot pepper sauce, salt, and pepper. Gradually add clam liquor and half and half. Cook, stirring constantly, until thick. Stir in lemon juice, parsley, pimiento, and clams. Pour mixture into a 9-inch round deep-dish pie plate (about 2 inches deep). Roll out pastry dough and place on top of mixture in pie plate; secure dough to the rim of the pie plate by crimping. Vent pastry. Brush with beaten egg. Bake in a hot oven, 375° F., for 25 to 30 minutes or until pastry is browned.

Makes 6 servings.

Claws

Face

Legs

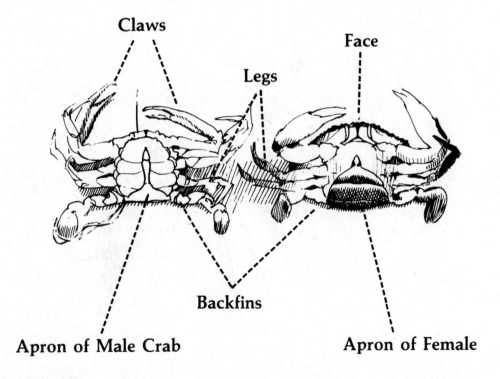

Backfins

Apron of Male Crab

Apron of Female

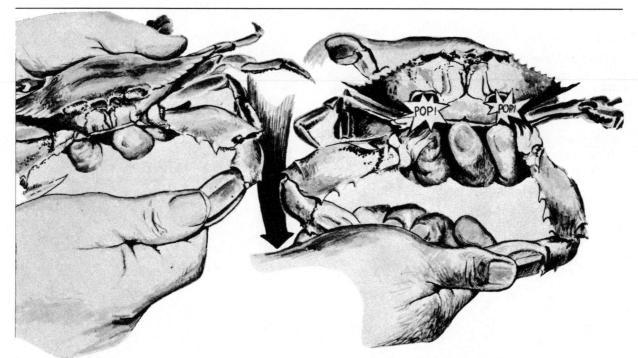

Holding crab in one hand, grip both claws with the other and pull down. Save claws.

Next, pull shell off the back. To do this hold backfin (A) with thumb and index finger of left hand and place either index finger or middle finger of the other hand under tip of shell (B) and flip off (C).

Some techniques recommend first pulling the apron off the bottom of the crab and then removing the shell. However, in the method illustrated the apron stays on while taking the crab apart because the apron supports the body.

There is some food inside the tips of the shell of larger crabs which is worth digging out.

Save shells for a dish for seafood. The method for cleaning them is described in the recipe section.

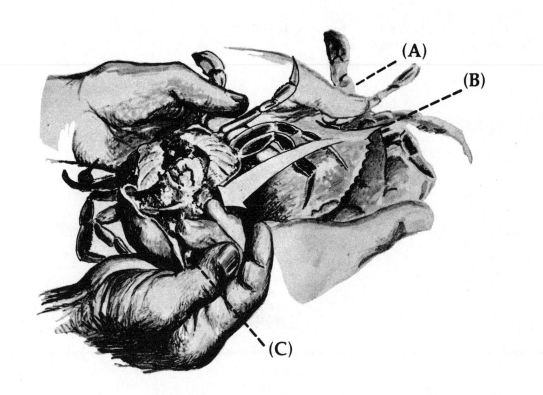

When the shell is off, you will see the so-called "devil's fingers" which are actually the gills of the crab. They are grayish-white and feathery.

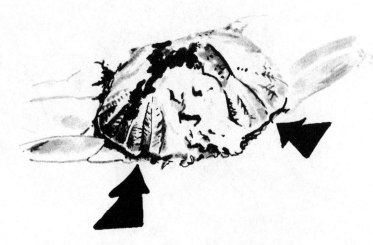

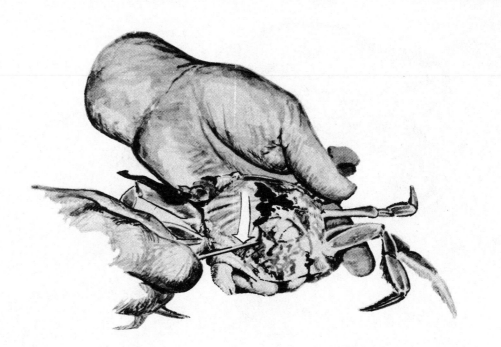

Scrape off gills from both sides of the crab.

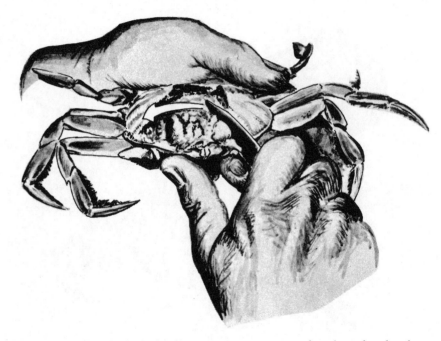

Cut out face with sharp knife or gouge out, using thumb and index finger.

Dislodge viscera. The yellow matter in the viscera is called crab butter. Some people find it to be delicious. It is really the crab's equivalent of a combination liver and pancreas.

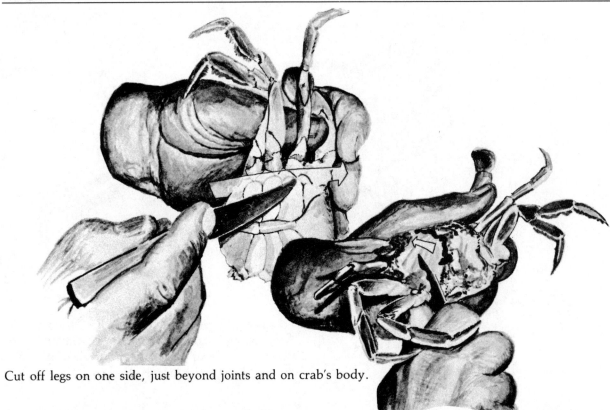

Cut off legs on one side, just beyond joints and on crab's body.

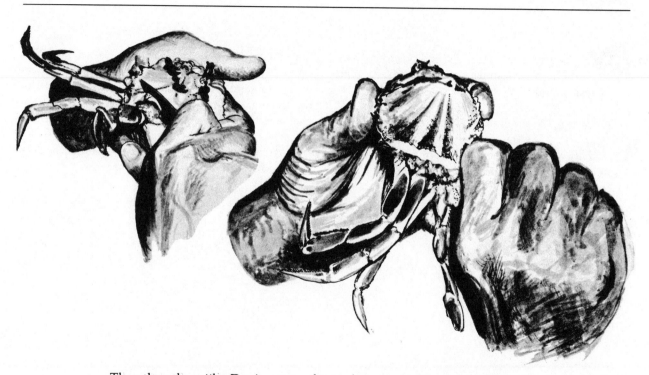

Then the other side. Don't cut too far in, because you'll cut into the meat.

This is the most crucial cut. The object is to lay bare the top and bottom chambers of the crab's body and to expose as much of the backfin as possible.

In drawing (A) the crab is held showing its left side. The backfin is to the right in the illustration. The curved arrow shows where you want to cut. The cut should be about a quarter of an inch behind a dark tinge on the crab's back as shown by dotted lines. This is the crab's collar bone. Cut down about halfway into the crab and then back toward you as is shown by the arrow in illustration (B). Take off the top section and save to pick out meat from the chambers later.

Next cut the other side of the crab—behind the dark tinge, down and back. Save top section.

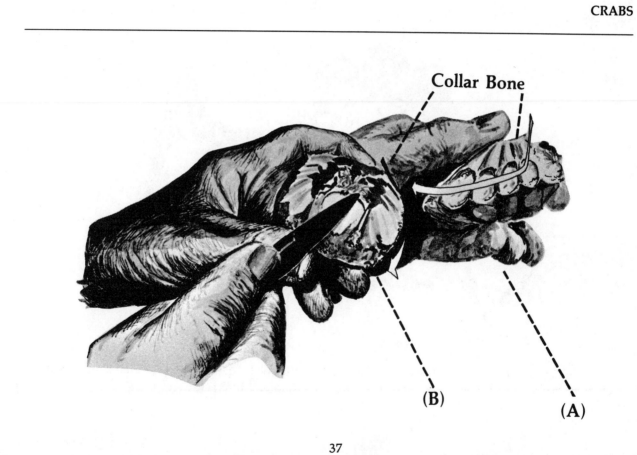

Collar Bone

(B)

(A)

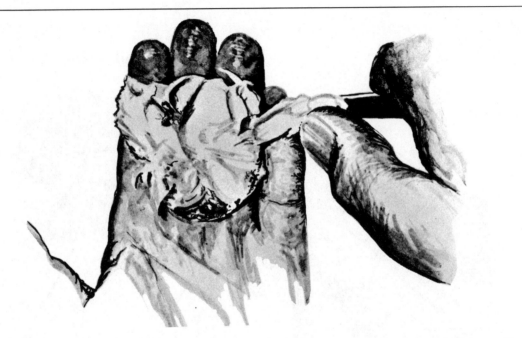

Using the pointed blade of the knife pick out as much of the backfin meat in one piece as possible. Do both sides.

Then pick out meat from the chambers of both the bottom and top sections of the shell.

As is shown in the section on lobster, it's possible to push back the movable claw of the crab's pinchers and hope that the meat will come out connected to the thin cartilage, but as one writer put it, the moon and the tide and all astrological signs have to be just right. The best way is shown at right. Crack the shell all the way around with the knife and then pull out as shown in next step. We've seen people put the claw in their mouth and in corn eating fashion crack the shell around with their teeth. This does draw attention. Notice that neither a mallet nor nut crackers were used. The mallet in the drawing in the beginning of this section is in case somebody wants to make a speech after eating the crabs.

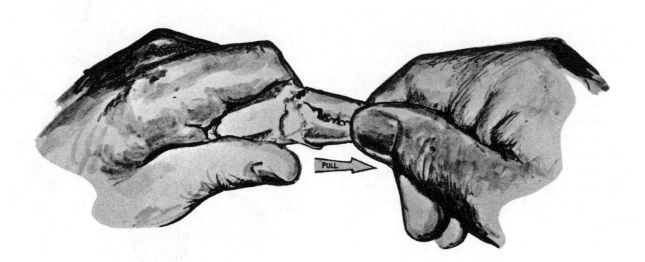

And pull out.

Crack around the joints behind the claw and pull out the meat.

Scissors and Knives are needed for
Soft Shell Blue Crabs

The blue crab is the most intricate of shellfish from which to collect meat, even though it obligingly turns soft so that nearly all of it can be eaten with only the minimum of preparation. Then scissors or a sharp knife are the implements to use.

Cut out the face. This is beheading the crab. With knife . . .

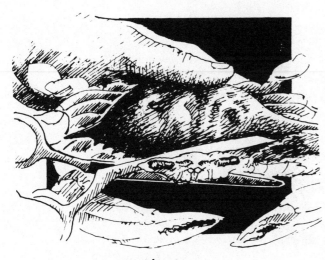

or with scissors.

Kill crab by sticking knife behind the eyes, then cut out face. Lift up the tips of the shells and scrape out gills or devil fingers as shown in step 3 of opening a hardshell crab. Next remove apron. Wash crab thoroughly.

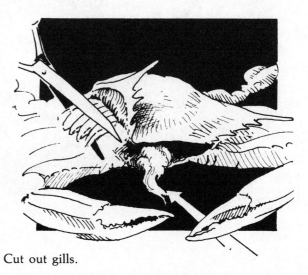

Cut out gills.

Cut away apron.

Cooking

Place crabs on their backs in frying pan with about ⅛ inch of hot oil and fry crabs in moderate heat. When crabs are brown on one side turn over and fry until brown on the other. This takes about 10 minutes.

These can be eaten as a sandwich with lettuce and mayonnaise, or with tartar sauce.

Other Crabs

It is now just as easy or even easier for people living along the Mid-Atlantic coast to purchase Dungeness crabs from the west coast, King Crab from Alaska and lobsters from Maine as it is to obtain oysters and clams in their shells. Thus, in a way, such shellfish are now "local."

Crabs, brought in from off the Atlantic Coast and elsewhere are being served in restaurants and sold in seafood markets in most parts of the country.

Some shell fish, like King Crab Legs and Dungeness crabs, are pre-cooked and arrive in stores frozen. Rinse in hot tap water for about five minutes, then steam for fifteen or twenty minutes. Or, you can let the meat thaw and cook right away. Warming the shellfish under hot tap water seems to free the meat from the shell.

There are other shellfish like periwinkles, hermit crabs, fiddler crabs and, yes (yuch), even horseshoe crabs that have edible and delicious meat. These would be treated like fresh blue crabs.

King Crabs

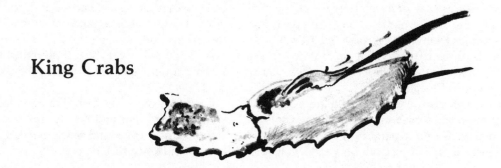

Usually the shell of the Alaskan King Crab is too soft to crack with the nut crackers which are normally provided at restaurants. Take the little fork used for picking out the meat and, working it like a can opener, go down one side, then the other.

Spread open the shell, take out the meat, and strip out the inedible cartilage. Nutcrackers can be used to open the harder shells and joints.

Dungeness Crabs

Dungeness crabs are named for an area in California and look like oversized blue crabs.

The best way to get the meat from Dungeness crabs is to break off the claws and crack with a mallet or nut cracker, then break the crab in half and knock body against a bowl and let the meat fall out. You may have to dig in with your fingers to break out some of the bone structure.

Rock/Jonah Crabs

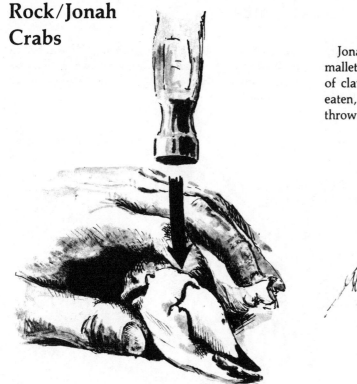

Jonah and Rock crabs are as hard as rocks. Here a mallet or hammer is necessary. Strike crown just back of claw, then pull out claw. Since only the claw is eaten, fishermen take crabs, break off one claw and throw the crab back. It will grow another to replace it.

Eat dipped in melted butter.

Red Crabs

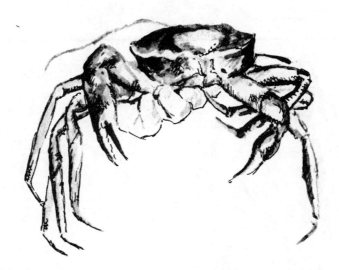

The body of a red crab can be eaten using the steps shown for dismantling a blue crab or it can be cut in half, as mentioned in the Dungeness crab section, and the meat knocked out. However, this is a little hard to do in a restaurant.

The most delicious meat of a red crab is in the legs and claws.

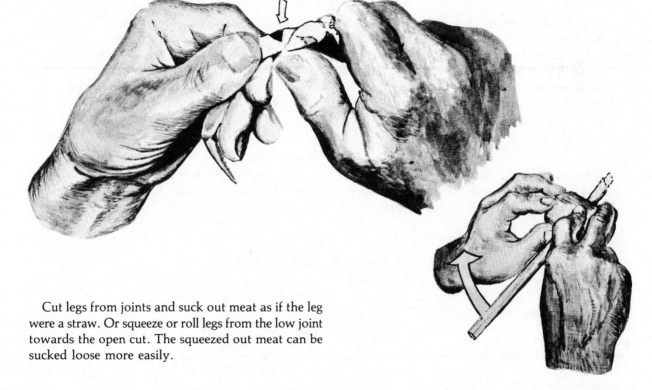

Cut legs from joints and suck out meat as if the leg were a straw. Or squeeze or roll legs from the low joint towards the open cut. The squeezed out meat can be sucked loose more easily.

Cooking Crabs

If possible, chill crabs in crushed ice until they are limp and then fold claws and legs under bodies. This numbs the crabs before they are cooked, relaxes the muscles, enhancing the texture of the meat, and makes them more compact in the pot.

Crabs should be steamed.

If you don't have a steamer or raised platform for your pot such as a trivet or colander, place two or three tablespoons of water in the bottom of the pot. Crabs are naturally moist, so the problem is to keep them from becoming too watery. Cover and steam crabs for about 30 minutes.

Serving

Some cynics say that the only purpose of newspaper is to wrap fish. This is not true. Newspapers are much better suited to serve as a table covering when eating crabs. Leave crab remains on the newspapers, then bundle remains, except for top shells, and place in nearest trash container.

Save Shells and Clean Them

Save your crab shells. This Neptune China makes unique dishes for Crab Imperial or crab salad.

Scrub shells with brush until clean. Cover shells with hot water in pot, add 1 teaspoon baking soda. Bring water to a boil, lower heat and let simmer for 20 minutes.

The Truly Maryland Way of Steamed Crabs

Whereas it's very easy to make cocktail sauce, it's cheaper and easier to buy already prepared seafood seasoning such as Old Bay (and many seafood restaurants sell their own home brand) than to make your own.

Mix seasoning, salt, vinegar and beer.

Put six crabs in large pot, followed by half the seasoning mixture, then the rest of the crabs and mixture. Cover tightly and steam crabs for 30 minutes.

¼ cup seafood seasoning
¼ cup salt—rock salt if possible
1 cup white vinegar
1 cup beer
12 crabs

Crab Imperial

Crab Imperial is more famous than the person it honored, Queen Henrietta Maria, wife of Charles I of England. Maryland was named for her.

3 tablespoons margarine or butter
1 tablespoon flour
½ cup milk
1 teaspoon minced onions
1½ teaspoon Worcestershire sauce
White bread cubed. 2 slices with crust removed
1 lb. crabmeat
½ cup mayonnaise
1 tablespoon lemon juice
1 egg beaten
½ teaspoon salt and few dashes of pepper
Paprika

Melt 1 tablespoon margarine or butter, mix in flour.

Slowly add milk, stirring constantly. Cook over medium heat, until mixture comes to boil and thickens.

Add onions, Worcestershire sauce and bread cubes and let cool.

In a separate pan, heat the remaining 2 tablespoons margarine or butter and crabmeat. Gently fold crabmeat into the sauce mixture. Spoon mixture into shells.

Make topping by stirring together mayonnaise, lemon juice, egg, salt and pepper, and spoon over filled shells. Sprinkle with paprika and bake at 450° F for about 10 minutes or until lightly brown on top.

Creamy Crab Chowder

2 tablespoons butter or margarine
4 green onions (cut up)
1 or 2 diced potatoes (according to size)
2 eggs
½ teaspoon Morton's Nature's Seasoning
2 or 3 teaspoons Old Bay Seasoning (according to taste)
2 or 3 dashes Worcestershire sauce
1 pound backfin crabmeat
32 ounces heavy cream
Juice of 2 or 3 lemons (according to size)
1 teaspoon chervil or dried parsley

In a 4-quart pot, melt butter or margarine and then saute onions on low heat until onions are tender. In a separate pot, half-filled with water, add potatoes and par boil for about 15 minutes. Add crabmeat to onions in the pot and continue slow saute.

In a separate bowl, whisk together eggs, Nature's Seasoning, Old Bay, and Worcestershire. Add this mixture to the crab and onions. Slowly add cream and bring to a boil. Drain the potatoes and add them and the lemon juice to the boiling mixture. Cover pot, and simmer for about 20 to 30 minutes, until the mixture thickens. Ladle into serving bowls and sprinkle on chervil or parsley.

Serves 4 to 6 people. Have a bowl of oyster crackers available for those who desire them. This chowder, when accompanied by a tossed salad, makes a complete meal in itself.

Crab Salad Sauce

1 cup catsup

1 cup mayonnaise

½ teaspoon garlic salt

½ teaspoon horseradish

½ teaspoon chopped sweet pickle

1 hard-boiled egg, minced or finely chopped

Mix all ingredients and chill

This sauce can also be used for shrimp.

King for a King

Meat from 12 crab legs

¼ cup butter

1 cup sliced mushrooms

dashes of salt and pepper

¼ cup sherry

Paprika

Saute crabmeat in butter for 3 minutes.

Add mushrooms and saute for 4 minutes. Add salt and pepper to taste.

Pour sherry over the mixture and light it. Shake pan until flame goes out.

Sprinkle crabmeat with paprika.

Tomato Crab Soup

1 cup sliced or chopped onion

2 tablespoons margarine or butter

1 tablespoon flour

1 can condensed tomato soup

1 quart half and half or milk

1 lb. crabmeat

¼ cup sherry

Saute onion in butter and stir in flour. Stir in tomato soup and half and half, and add crabmeat. Heat, don't boil. Add sherry and serve.

Note: For another crab soup which requires a little more time, see recipe for whelk chowder on page 130.

Crab Louis

1 pound Dungeness crabmeat, or other crabmeat, fresh frozen, or pasteurized
½ pound Dungeness or King Crab legs or other crab legs, fresh or frozen
Salad greens
1½ quarts shredded salad greens
1 cup mayonnaise or salad dressing
¼ cup chili sauce
2 tablespoons finely chopped green pepper
2 tablespoons finely chopped onion
2 tablespoons finely chopped parsley
⅛ teaspoon cayenne pepper
¼ cup whipping cream, whipped
2 hard-cooked eggs, quartered
2 tomatoes, quartered
Ripe olives
Parsley sprigs
Lemon wedges

Thaw crabmeat if frozen. Drain crabmeat. Remove any remaining pieces of shell or cartilage.

Line salad plates or bowls with salad greens; fill with shredded salad greens. Mound body crabmeat on lettuce. Combine mayonnaise, chili sauce, green pepper, onion, parsley and cayenne. Fold in whipped cream. Pour sauce over crabmeat.

Garnish plates with crab legs, eggs, tomatoes, olives, parsley, and lemon wedges.

Makes 4 servings.

Maryland Deviled Crab

1 pound crabmeat, fresh, frozen, or pasteurized
2 tablespoons margarine or butter
½ cup finely chopped onion
¼ cup finely chopped green pepper
¼ cup all purpose flour
1 tablespoon dry mustard
1 teaspoon Worcestershire sauce
¾ teaspoon salt
¼ teaspoon liquid hot pepper sauce
¼ teaspoon pepper
Dash cayenne, optional
1¼ cups half and half
2 egg yolks, beaten
½ cup fresh bread crumbs
½ teaspoon paprika
1 tablespoon margarine or butter
Lemon wedges

Thaw crabmeat if frozen. Remove any remaining shell or cartilage. In a large skillet melt margarine. Add onion and green pepper and cook until vegetables are tender. Stir in flour, mustard, Worcestershire, liquid hot pepper sauce, salt, pepper, and cayenne. Add half and half gradually. Cook over low heat until thickened, stirring constantly. Add a little of the hot sauce to egg yolks; add to remaining sauce, stirring constantly. Place crab mixture into 6 crab shells or ramekins. Combine bread crumbs, paprika, and margarine. Sprinkle on top of crab mixture. Bake in a moderate oven, 350° F., for 15 to 20 minutes or until hot and bread crumbs are browned. Serve with lemon wedges. Makes 6 servings.

Note: If desired, mixture may be chilled and shaped into 6 crab cakes. Dip in crumbs and fry in oil ⅛ inch deep in a skillet until golden brown on both sides.

Astoria Deviled Crab

1 package (6 ounces) snow crab or other crabmeat, fresh or frozen

or

1 can (6½ ounces) crabmeat
1 can (4 ounces) mushroom stems and pieces, undrained
2 hard-cooked eggs, chopped
½ cup finely chopped green pepper
1 jar (2 ounces) pimiento strips, undrained
1 tablespoon catsup
1 teaspoon Worcestershire sauce
1 cup thick white sauce
1 package (4¾ ounces) or 2 cups potato chips, crushed
¼ teaspoon salt
⅛ teaspoon pepper
3 tablespoons margarine or butter
¼ cup grated Parmesan cheese
Paprika
Lemon slices

Thaw crabmeat if frozen. Drain canned crabmeat. Remove any remaining shell or cartilage. Combine crabmeat with remaining ingredients except margarine, cheese, paprika, and lemon slices.

Place crab mixture in a well-greased baking dish, 11½ × 7 × 1¾ inches. Dot with margarine and sprinkle with cheese and paprika. Place lemon slices on top of casserole.

Bake in a hot oven, 400° F., for 15 to 20 minutes.

Makes 6 servings.

Crab Chops

1 pound blue crabmeat, fresh, frozen, or pasteurized
¼ cup margarine or butter
¼ cup all-purpose flour
½ teaspoon salt
¼ teaspoon cayenne pepper
1 cup milk
¼ cup chopped parsley
¼ cup chopped green onion
½ cup all-purpose flour
2 eggs, beaten
2 cups soft bread crumbs
¼ cup margarine or butter
¼ cup cooking oil
Lemon wedges
Tartar sauce

Thaw crabmeat if frozen. Remove any remaining shell or cartilage from crabmeat. In small saucepan melt ¼ cup margarine; blend in ¼ cup flour, salt, and cayenne. Gradually stir in milk. Cook and stir until thickened. Mix in crabmeat, parsley, and green onion. Cover and refrigerate for 2 hours.

Divide crab mixture into 6 equal portions. Pat and shape each portion into a "chop" about 5 inches long and ½ inch thick. Place each chop in the ½ cup flour and turn to coat both sides. Dip each chop into egg and then turn in the bread crumbs to coat evenly. Refrigerate at least 30 minutes to firm coating.

In heavy 12-inch fry pan, heat ¼ cup margarine and ¼ cup oil until hot but not smoking. Fry chops over moderate heat until delicately browned on both sides, about 10 minutes. Serve with lemon wedges and tartar sauce.

Makes 6 servings.

Cornish Crab

1 package (6 ounces) snow crab or other crabmeat, fresh or frozen

or

1 can (6½ ounces) crabmeat
4 large baked potatoes
½ cup margarine or butter, softened
¼ cup milk
½ teaspoon salt
¼ teaspoon pepper
¼ teaspoon paprika
Parsley
Lemon wedges

Thaw crabmeat if frozen. Drain canned crabmeat. Remove any remaining shell or cartilage. Cut a slice off the top of each potato; scoop out potatoes, reserving shells. Mash potatoes; stir in margarine, milk, salt, and pepper. Beat until fluffy. fold in crabmeat. Stuff potato shells with crab and potato mixture. Sprinkle stuffed potatoes with paprika.

Bake in a hot oven, 400° F., for 10 to 15 minutes, or until hot and lightly browned. Garnish with parsley sprigs and lemon wedges.

Makes 4 servings.

Never let steamed crabs come in contact with any surfaces, baskets or containers that have held uncooked crabs. Bacteria will spread like wild fire.

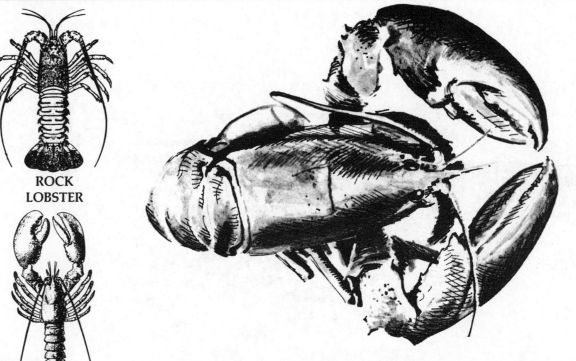

ROCK LOBSTER

AMERICAN LOBSTER

Lobster is so expensive that not one shred of it should be wasted.

If you're cooking the lobster yourself, after removing it from the steamer cut the lobster from stem to stern, through the tail and body. If bought in restaurants, the lobster will probably arrive at your table cut. For killing and cooking lobster see page 74.

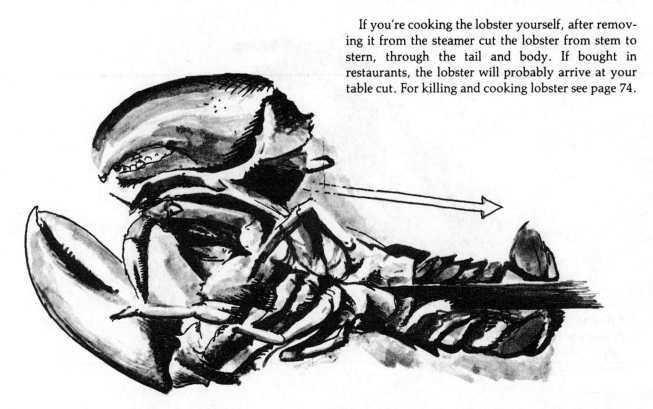

First twist off claws, put them aside. Then break off tail section. There is enough similarity between these tails and the frozen lobster tails (which are actually crayfish) you buy at stores, that you can open them the same way.

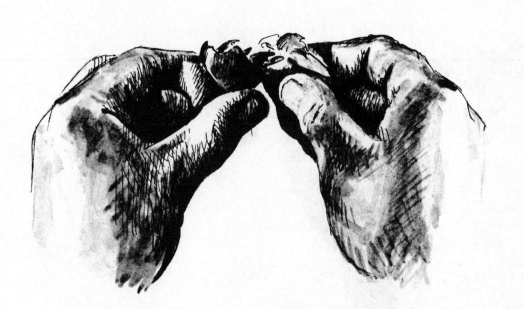

Break off the fan at very end of tail. If the lobster is big enough there are particles of meat in each of the fins of the fan worth going after.

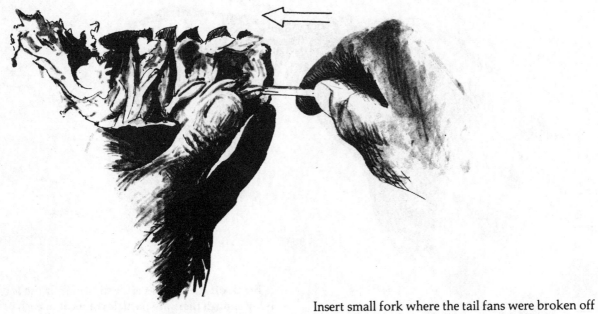

Insert small fork where the tail fans were broken off
and push out the meat from tail in one piece.

Pull back section from the body.

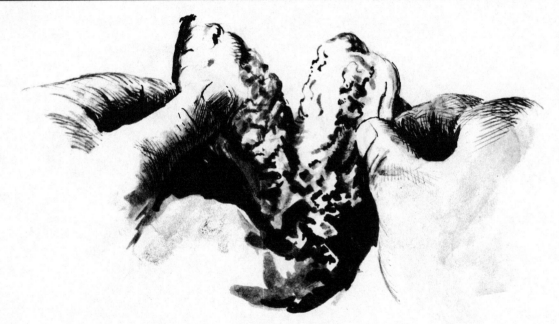

Open body. Pick out meat, but don't eat the feathery part.

The red coral and greenish liver, or tomally, can be mixed together. Add a few drops of lemon juice and dip the mixture in melted butter.

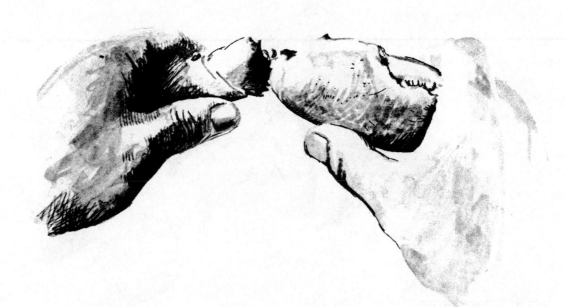

Take claw and break back against hinge.

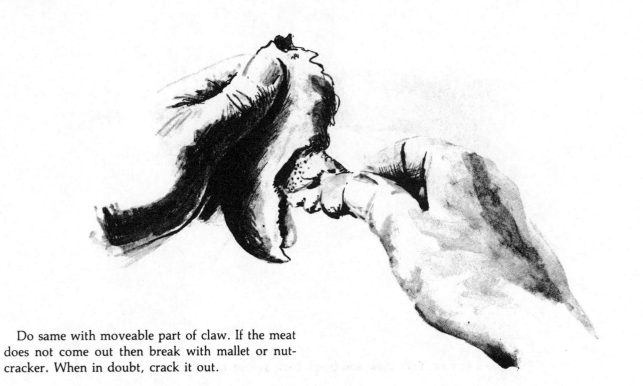

Do same with moveable part of claw. If the meat
does not come out then break with mallet or nut-
cracker. When in doubt, crack it out.

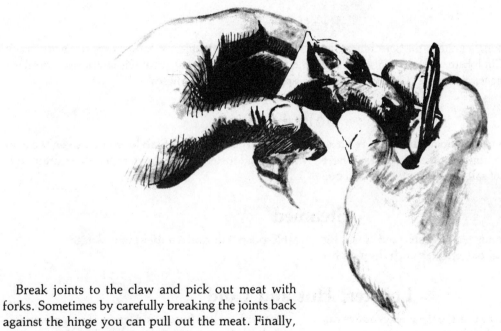

Break joints to the claw and pick out meat with forks. Sometimes by carefully breaking the joints back against the hinge you can pull out the meat. Finally, suck out the meat from the legs.

Lobster can be broiled, boiled, or steamed.

Broiled

Kill lobster by sticking a knife in the back where the tail and body meet. Cut lobster as shown in step 1 and discard small hard sac near the eyes. Cut away membrane from both sides of tail to expose meat. Crack claws and joints, brush meat with butter and broil for approximately 20 minutes.

Boiled

If rubber bands are used to hold claws shut, remove. Plunge lobster into boiling sea water or fresh water with one tablespoon of salt per quart of water and boil for exactly 20 minutes. Stab lobster between the eyes and hang lobster upside down to let water drain out.

Steamed

Remove rubber bands from lobster and steam for 20 minutes in water about one half inch deep with 1 tablespoon salt and 1 tablespoon vinegar.

Lobster, Hot and Cold

Lobster prepared in any of the three ways above can be served either hot or cold. Hot with melted butter and lemon if you prefer and chilled with mayonnaise, preferably homemade.

Lobster Salad

1 pound cooked spiny lobster meat, fresh or frozen

6 hard cooked eggs

½ cup salad oil

1 tablespoon sugar

1 teaspoon dry mustard

1 teaspoon salt

¼ teaspoon cayenne pepper

½ cup vinegar

1½ cups chopped celery

1½ cups chopped green onion

2 tablespoons capers with liquid

Salad greens

Thaw lobster meat if frozen. Cut meat into ½ inch cubes.

Peel eggs; separate whites and yolks. Sieve or mash the egg yolks; gradually blend in oil. Stir sugar, mustard, salt, and pepper into vinegar. Combine with egg yolks. Set aside.

Chop egg whites. Combine lobster meat, celery, egg whites, green onion, and capers. Pour dressing over salad and mix lightly. Serve on salad greens.

Makes 6 servings.

Lobster Thermidor

3 live lobsters (about 1¾ pounds each)
⅓ cup margarine or butter
1½ cups chopped fresh mushrooms
3 tablespoons minced onion
1½ tablespoons all-purpose flour
¼ teaspoon liquid hot pepper sauce
¾ teaspoon salt
1½ cups half and half
3 egg yolks, beaten
3 tablespoons brandy
2 tablespoons chopped parsley
3 tablespoons fresh bread crumbs
3 tablespoons grated parmesan cheese
½ teaspoon paprika
1 tablespoon melted margarine or butter

Place lobsters, head first, into a large pot of boiling water. Cover and simmer 15 to 20 minutes until lobsters are done. Legs will twist off easily when done. Remove lobsters from pot. Cut off antennae. Twist off claws of lobster. Crack and remove meat. Using scissors cut through the soft stomach shell; remove the tail meat being careful to keep shells intact. Save the red coral roe, if any. Discard the stomach; set aside the shells. Cut the lobster meat into ½ inch cubes and set aside.

In a skillet melt margarine. Add mushrooms and onion and cook until tender. Stir flour, liquid hot pepper sauce, and salt. Gradually blend in half and half. Cook, stirring constantly until thick. Add a little hot sauce to egg yolks; add to remaining sauce, stirring constantly. Heat until thickened. Stir in brandy, parsley, reserved lobster meat, and red coral roe, if any. Divide lobster mixture into shells or ramekins. Place shells on a baking tray. Combine bread crumbs, parmesan cheese, paprika, and margarine. Sprinkle crumb mixture over lobsters. Bake in a moderate oven, 350° F., for 15 to 20 minutes or until hot.

Makes 6 servings.

The Basic Oysters

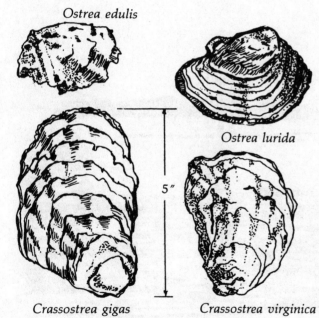

Ostrea edulis

Ostrea lurida

Crassostrea gigas

Crassostrea virginica

5"

Scientific name	Common name(s)	Locality
Crassostrea virginica	American	Native of east coast of United States
Ostrea lurida	Olympia, Yaquina	Native of west coast of United States
Crassostrea gigas	Pacific, Kuma-moto	Japan, now in Pacific Northwest
Ostrea edulis	European	Europe

Oysters are the hardest and riskiest of all shellfish to open. Still, style is very important. As in dismantling a lobster, you are rated by performance and you can easily lower your rating by slipping and sending the blade of your oyster knife through your hand. Never let one hand be where the blade of the knife could be!

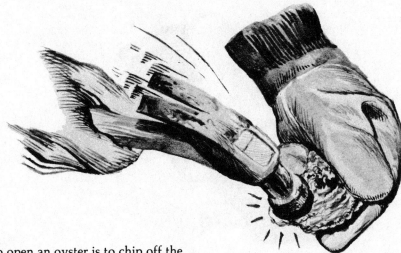

The fastest way to open an oyster is to chip off the thin lip with a hammer or any hard object—even the back of a spoon—until . . .

. . . you have a small opening. The opening shown
is slightly exaggerated.

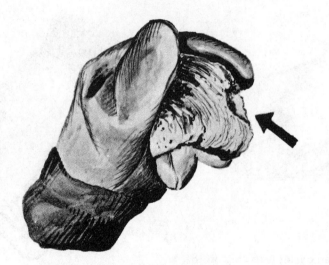

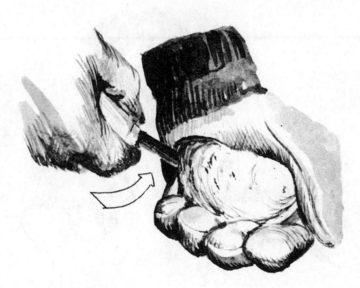

Slip in blade, cut muscles and scoop oysters free from shell. This method of shucking is called breaking the oyster.

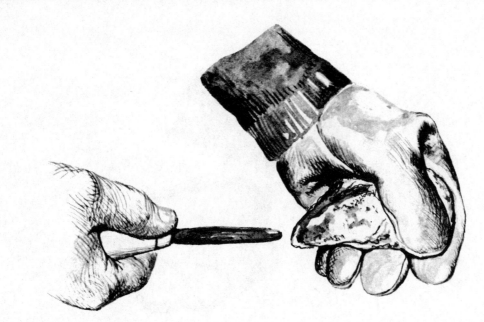

For smaller oysters you can open from the front, as shown, and actually pop them open. This requires practice and a strong wrist, but once perfected is the fastest method and is also the one which leaves the oyster most free of pieces of shell.

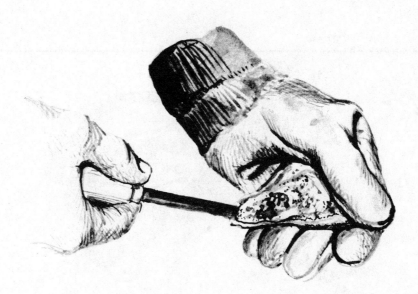

Work the oyster knife into the front. On the larger
oyster you can go in deep and cut the muscle.

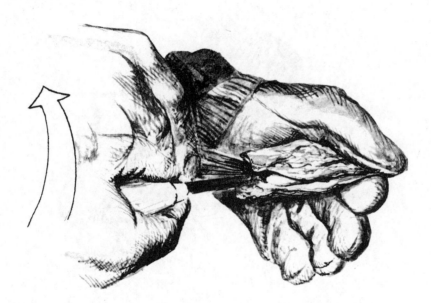

Then twist and pop the oyster open.

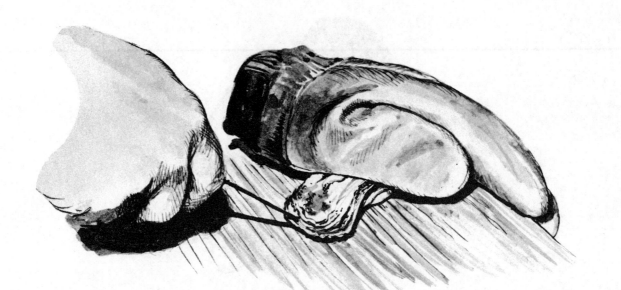

Another method is to stab the oyster. This is done with large and thick-shelled oysters. Hold the oyster down with the flat of your hand and work the blade in through the bivalves either from the sides or front. This requires more familiarity with the oyster than the other methods.

Then open it and cut meat free.

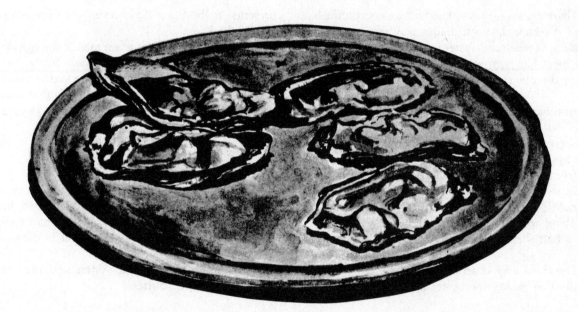

Arranged on a tray, oysters can be "riding" on the top shell, in which case they appear larger, or settled in the bottom half of the shell in their own juice. Either way they should be set on a bed of crushed ice, accompanied with wedges of lemons and/or a sauce such as the one mentioned on page 15.

There are three ways of serving oysters on the half shell. Perhaps the most unique way, but common in Britain, is when the oyster is in the bottom shell and the meat has been severed and flipped over. In this way, the oyster presents "its best face."

Another method is having the oyster in its bottom shell but unturned. Sometimes in France, the oyster is not severed from its shell. This way the eater knows the oyster belongs to the shell and hasn't been slipped in from a can to an old shell. Also, the oyster maintains its appearance of being alive longer—about 10 minutes; 5 minutes if the oyster has been severed. Nothing appears flatter than an oyster that has been on a half shell too long.

The third way is serving the oyster on the upper shell. This makes the oyster appear larger and also presents "its best face." However, the juice is lost in this method.

It's been said that the bravest man in the world was the first man who ate an oyster. More likely, he was one of the hungriest. However, if he had known that raw oysters were one of the few foods that reaches your mouth still alive and is eventually killed by gastric juices . . . ?

Broiled with Bacon

Here's a quick recipe, if you've decided not to have raw oysters. Fill the oysters with seasoned bread crumbs and on each oyster place a strip of bacon which can be the length of the oyster. Broil in oven until bacon is crisp.

You can also bake or grill oysters until they open, then dip in melted butter.

Oysters Rockefeller

1 pint oysters, selects or counts, fresh or frozen
¼ cup margarine or butter
¼ cup chopped celery
¼ cup chopped green onion
2 tablespoons chopped parsley
1 package (10 ounces) frozen chopped spinach
1 tablespoon anisette
¼ teaspoon salt
Rock salt
18 baking shells
¼ cup dry bread crumbs
1 tablespoon melted margarine or butter

Thaw oysters if frozen. In small saucepan melt ¼ cup margarine. Add celery, green onion, and parsley.

Cover and cook 5 minutes or until tender. Combine cooked vegetables with spinach in blender container. Add anisette and salt. Chop vegetables in blender until almost pureed, stopping once or twice to push vegetables into knife blades. (Vegetables may be run through a food mill.) Make a layer of rock salt in pie tins. Place small baking shells or ramekins on top. (The rock salt is used mainly to hold shells upright; however, it also helps to keep oysters hot to serve.) Place the oysters in the shells or ramekins. Top each oyster with spinach mixture. Combine bread crumbs and 1 tablespoon melted margarine; sprinkle over oysters. Bake in a very hot oven, 450° F., for 10 minutes. Serve immediately in pie tins.

Makes 6 appetizer servings of 3 oysters each.

Oysters Robinson

Antoine's in New Orleans, Louisiana is famous for its Oysters Rockefeller, but it's becoming just as well known because it does not add spinach to its recipe. The only part of the recipe which the restaurant reveals is what it doesn't put into it. That's spinach. But this turns out to be very important and after you try the following recipe, you may never try spinach again. Also, you won't try to figure out what's in the Antoine's recipe.

If you are unaware of the story behind Oysters Rockefeller, it was a dish created to replace snails with the plentiful oysters. Because the sauce was so rich, the owner of the restaurant named it after the richest man he could think of. It's a good thing this all happened when it did. Can you imagine Oysters Getty or Oysters Onassis?

The following recipe is called Oysters Robinson, subtitled "The Poor Man's Oysters Rockefeller."

2 cups chopped collard or turnip greens or
2 cups chopped watercress or wintercress
1 cup chopped onions
¼ cup chopped celery
½ cup parsley
1 teaspoon dried tarragon leaves
2 sticks butter
½ cup dry bread crumbs
½ cup Anisette
2 dozen oysters on the half-shell

If you are using collard or turnip greens, boil them in water for one minute and then rinse in cold water. This process "sweetens" them. When measuring greens, press them into the cups, but do not pack them.

Saute the onions and celery in four tablespoons of butter for about three minutes. Add the greens, parsley, and tarragon, and stir until wilted, which should be a few minutes. Combine this mixture with the rest of the butter, bread crumbs, and Anisette. Place in blender and process until smooth.

Place the oysters on rock salt or arrange them on crimpled tin foil to keep them in place. Carefully spoon sauce on top of oysters. Bake at 475° F until butter is melted and oysters are warm.

Oyster Stew

A customer was complaining quite loudly to a friend about the sparse portions of food in a restaurant, when he was overheard by the owner who warned if he didn't quiet down, he would dump a bowl of oyster stew on the customer's head.

You can tell what kind of restaurant this was.

"No, you won't dump the oyster stew on my head," the customer said. "And for two reasons. One is that you don't want to waste the stew and second you don't want the other customers to see that there's only three oysters in it."

If there is a moral to the story it's that you should add lots of oysters to an oyster stew.

The quality of an oyster stew is determined not only by the number of oysters in it, but by the degree of bitter cold outside and chill in your bones. Unfortunately, unless you open your own oysters, you cannot usually buy "dirty" (a term meaning freshly shucked oysters in their own juice) oysters in stores.

1 quart milk or half & half
1½ pint oysters
1 ounce clam juice
salt and white pepper
dash cayenne pepper
Paprika
Butter (optional)

Heat milk but don't boil.

Add oysters and juice (oyster or clam) and cook until the edges on oysters curl.

Season with the peppers and salt.

Pour into heated bowls and sprinkle on paprika. Add pats (about 2 tablespoons) of butter if you like.

Although there are various legends about the origin of the Hangtown Fry, most seem to agree that the incident occurred in 1849, at Hangtown, California, involved a miner, and utilized eggs and Olympia oysters. One version tells of a miner condemned to hang, who requested as his last meal, eggs scrambled with Olympia oysters. Consequently a stay of execution was granted until the oysters could be obtained from Puget Sound, two states north. As the story goes—the condemned man was rescued by his pals before the oysters arrived. However, the marshall endorsed the dish after the oysters arrived and Hangtown Fry became a favorite dish among the miners. A California version of this yarn tells of a successful gold miner who had struck it rich, hailed into Hangtown, and ordered the finest, most expensive meal available, which happened to be Olympia oysters and eggs.

Hangtown Fry

1 can (12 ounces) medium Pacific oysters, fresh or frozen
3 slices bacon, cut in 1-inch pieces
8 eggs
¼ cup water
½ teaspoon salt
Dash of pepper
½ cup dry bread or cracker crumbs
⅓ cup flour
¼ cup milk
2 tablespoons melted margarine or cooking oil
2 teaspoons minced parsley
Lemon wedges

Thaw oysters if frozen; drain. Fry bacon in 10-inch frypan until crisp. Drain on absorbent paper. Reserve bacon drippings. Combine eggs, water, salt, and pepper; beat slightly, set aside. Combine and mix crumbs and flour. Dip oysters in milk; roll in crumb mixture.

Heat margarine and reserved bacon drippings in frypan. Fry oysters in hot fat over moderate heat for 2 or 3 minutes or until lightly browned. Sprinkle crisp bacon pieces over oysters. Pour egg mixture over bacon and oysters. Cook over low heat.

Gently lift edge of omelet with spatula to allow uncooked egg to flow to bottom of pan. Cook just until eggs are set. Sprinkle with parsley before serving. If preferred, loosen omelet around edge of pan; fold and roll onto heated platter and sprinkle with parsley. Serve with lemon wedges.

Makes 6 servings.

Early 20th Century Advertising Card

Oyster Pie Rappahannock

1 pint oysters, standards, fresh or frozen
6 slices bacon
2 cups sliced fresh mushrooms
½ cup chopped onion
½ cup chopped green onion
¼ cup all-purpose flour
½ teaspoon salt
¼ teaspoon cayenne pepper
¼ cup chopped parsley
2 tablespoons lemon juice
1 tablespoon softened margarine or butter
Biscuit Topping

Thaw oysters if frozen. Drain oysters; dry between absorbent paper.

In a 10-inch fry pan cook bacon until crisp. Remove bacon, drain, and crumble. Reserve 3 tablespoons bacon fat. Add mushrooms, onion, and green onion to reserved bacon fat.

Cover and simmer 5 minutes or until tender. Blend in flour, salt, and pepper. Stir in oysters, bacon, parsley, and lemon juice.

Grease a 9-inch pie plate with softened margarine. Turn oyster mixture into pie plate. Cover with biscuit topping. Score biscuit topping to make a design on top. Bake in very hot oven, 400° F., for 20 to 25 minutes or until biscuit topping is lightly browned. Cut into wedges.

Makes 6 servings.

By the middle of the 19th century, even away from the coastal regions, oysters were as popular with Americans as hot dogs are today. An entry from the diary of a St. Louis girl in the late 19th century reads ". . . oysters and other shellfish come by boat from New Orleans in barrels, and when a family is fortunate enough to get a barrel, all their friends are invited for the evening . . . what a treat this is considered!"

The codfish is one of the only foodstuffs that has been honored for its part in bringing prosperity to this country. In 1784, a four foot, eleven inch painted wooden codfish was hung in Old Boston State House. This symbol, which still hangs, was dedicated as follows: "A memorial to the importance of the cod-fishery to the welfare of this Commonwealth."

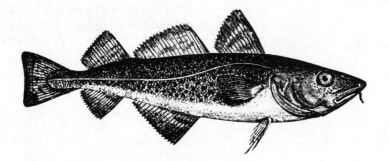

Cod and Oyster Scallop

1 pound cod fillets or other fish fillets, fresh or frozen
1 pint oysters, drained, fresh or frozen
½ cup margarine or butter
2 tablespoons finely chopped onion
¼ teaspoon liquid hot pepper sauce
3 cups crushed saltine crackers
2 tablespoons chopped parsley
¼ teaspoon salt
⅛ teaspoon pepper
1 cup half and half

Thaw fish and oysters if frozen. Cut fish into 1-inch cubes. In a saucepan melt margarine. Add onion and cook until tender. Stir in liquid hot pepper sauce.

Combine cooked vegetables, crackers, and parsley. Place ⅓ of crumb mixture in bottom of a well-greased 1½ quart casserole. Place ½ the fish and oysters on top of crumb mixture. Sprinkle with ½ the salt and pepper. Repeat layers ending with crumb mixture. Pour the half and half over contents in dish.

Bake in a hot oven, 400° F., for 25 to 30 minutes or until fish flakes easily when tested with a fork.

Makes 6 servings.

Oyster Loaf

1 pint oysters, standards, fresh or frozen
½ teaspoon salt
⅛ teaspoon pepper
2 eggs, beaten
¼ cup milk
¾ cup all-purpose flour
2 cups soft bread crumbs
½ cup melted margarine or butter
2 loaves French bread, 15 inches long and 3 inches wide
Fat for deep frying
½ cup tartar sauce
1½ cups shredded lettuce
18 thin tomato slices

Thaw oysters if frozen. Drain oysters; dry between absorbent paper. Sprinkle with salt and pepper. Combine eggs and milk. Roll oysters in flour, dip into egg mixture, then roll in bread crumbs to coat evenly.

Refrigerate at least 30 minutes to firm coating.

Slice bread loaves in half horizontally. Pull out the inside soft crumb from bottom and top halves of bread. Brush the bread shells inside with melted margarine. Place bread shells on baking sheet and bake in a moderate oven, 350° F., 3 to 5 minutes to warm and crisp.

Place oysters in a single layer in a fry basket. Fry in deep fat, 350° F., for 2 to 3 minutes. Drain on absorbent paper. Spread inside of bread shells with tartar sauce. Place shredded lettuce in the bottom halves of the loaves. Arrange tomato slices on lettuce, and fried oysters on top of the tomatoes. Cover with top halves of the loaves of bread. Cut each loaf into 3 portions.

Makes 6 servings.

The following three recipes (1904-1916) are from
"The Ladies of the Presbyterian Church, Lewes, Delaware."

Deviled Oysters

25 nice fat oysters
½ pint cream
1 tablespoon butter
2 tablespoons flour
1 tablespoon chopped parsley
yolks of 2 eggs
pepper and salt to taste
a little cayenne pepper

Drain the oysters, chop and drain again, put cream on to boil, rub butter and flour together, stir this in the boiling milk. As soon as it thickens remove from the fire.

Add all the other ingredients, the yolks well beaten. Fill the large shells with the mixture, sprinkle with bread crumbs; put a little piece of butter on top of each and brown.

Oyster Patties

1 quart oysters
1 pint sweet milk
1 tablespoon butter
1 tablespoon flour

Rub together the butter and flour. Add this to the hot milk and stir constantly until it thickens; then add the oysters, cook until the edges curl slightly.

Serve immediately after the shells are filled.

Oyster Croquettes

Boil twenty fine oysters in their own liquor for 5 minutes, stirring constantly, remove from the fire and drain. Chop the oysters into small pieces, then put into a saucepan one gill of the liquor and one of cream. When hot stir in one tablespoon of butter and two of flour that have previously been rubbed to a cream and stir till the mixture boils and thickens. Drop in the yolks of two eggs and stir for one minute longer, remove from the fire and add one tablespoon of chopped parsley and ¼ tablespoon nutmeg; salt and pepper to taste.

Turn out on a dish, when cold form into shape, roll in beaten egg and cracker or bread crumbs, and fry in smoking fat. Drain on coarse brown paper, garnish with parsley.

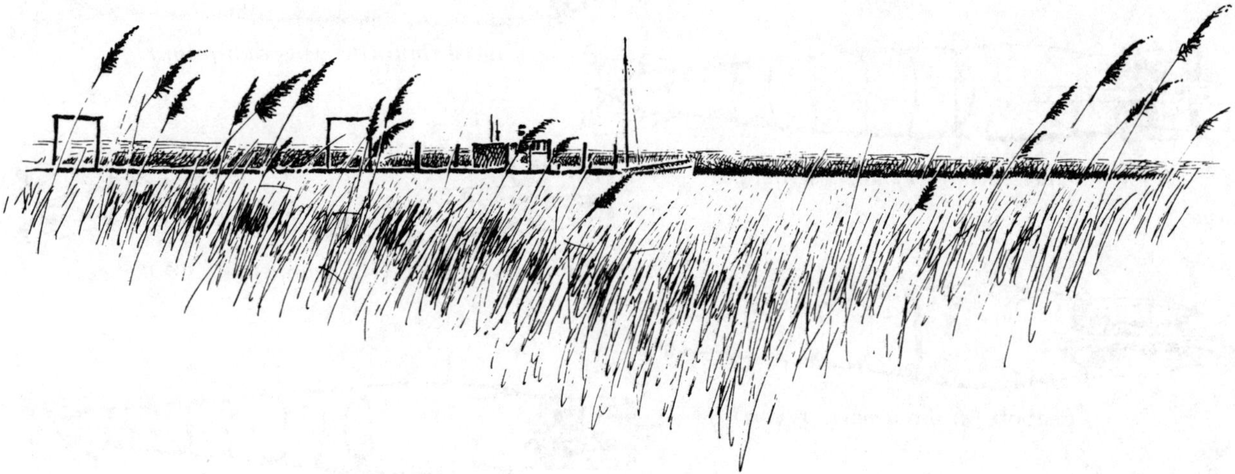

Various Commercial Shrimp

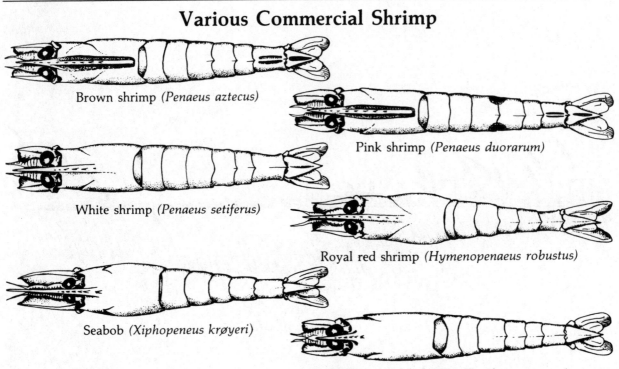

Brown shrimp *(Penaeus aztecus)*

Pink shrimp *(Penaeus duorarum)*

White shrimp *(Penaeus setiferus)*

Royal red shrimp *(Hymenopenaeus robustus)*

Seabob *(Xiphopeneus krøyeri)*

Broken-necked shrimp *(Trachypeneus sp.)*

Shelling Shrimp

Someone once said that it takes longer to explain how to clean a shrimp than it does to clean one. One writer, however, succinctly described the process as, "You shell a shrimp as you would a peanut." You would have to be able to peel a shrimp fast to race this description.

The Japanese have a unique method of cleaning shrimp which saves on fuel. They peel the shrimp live and while it is still kicking dip it in a sauce and then eat it. It's reportedly better if the shrimp is still wiggling than if it has been stilled by death. This is a custom that will surely stay in Japan.

In his *Long Island Seafood Cook Book*, published in 1939, J. George Frederick reports, "The quaintly imaginative yet practical Chinese, who are very fond of shrimp, talk about shrimps punished with bamboo, by which they mean an efficiency method they use to shell shrimp. They put the cooked shrimp in a bag and whip it with a bamboo rod, which loosens the shells from the shrimp in jig time."

Then there is the method of loosening the shells from the shrimp by tramping on them. This is a method probably no longer used.

Unlike most other shellfish, your hands are adequate implements for opening shrimp. Hold the tail in one hand and slip your thumb of your other hand under the shell between the swimmerettes and lift each section of the shell. When you reach the tail, pinch out the meat.

If the shrimp are large and the vein appears to have sand (or if you don't like the appearance of the vein) devein it with a knife or a toothpick. The beak of a beer can opener does an adequate job, too.

It's easier to clean raw shrimp than cooked, but shrimp cooked in their shells usually have a more natural curve, a bit more taste and richer pink color. So there you are. Gain on one and lose on the other.

Using a knife is faster than using hands. Peel the shrimp as you would an apple. Hold shrimp with your left hand with the swimmerettes or underside facing at an upward angle away from you. With your right hand place the blade of the knife along the inside of the swimmerettes on the top or nearest you . . .

Using a Knife on Shrimp

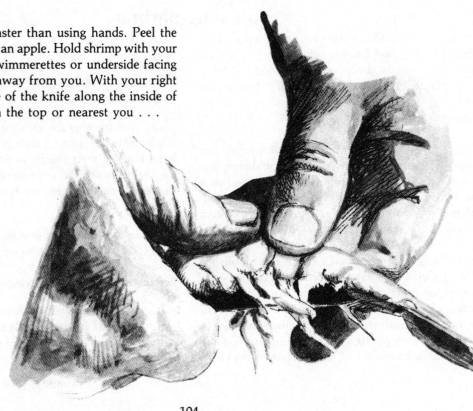

. . . then with your left hand turn the shrimp away from you while cutting under the swimmerettes and shell, which should start to peel.

105

Keep twisting and turning until the shell is off. Then pinch out the meat from the shell with your right hand. This can be done in one motion.

There. The shell is off.

Drop the shell and then with your left hand point the tail of the shrimp to your right hand and using your thumb and one of your fingers pinch out the meat from the tail.

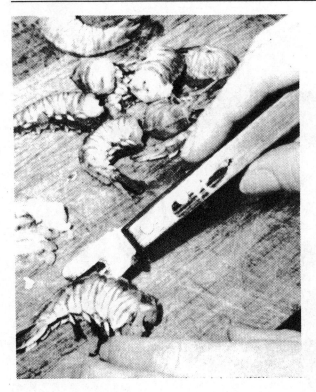

Rock Shrimp

Probably the most tedious shellfish to open are rock shrimp. Place each shrimp on a hard surface with its curved back up and whack with the handle of a knife or some other hard object. Then turn it over and keep hitting it. This breaks and loosens the shell so that you can peel it off. You should never try to shell these armored little creatures as you would the more familiar shrimp. You will cut your fingers. Also, don't try to use a shrimp cleaner because the rock shrimp would appear as if it had exploded in your hand.

One positive characteristic of rock shrimp is that its hard shell holds the shrimp in one piece so you can pry it loose from its frozen container. A regular shrimp would break into pieces.

The one drawback of these shrimp is that their veins are central and more pronounced, more like a string than a thread. The veins definitely have to be removed and the cavities flushed out.

The texture and taste of rock shrimp resembles the body section of lobsters and should be treated as such. You wouldn't dip lobster in a strong cocktail sauce, nor would you these shrimp. If the shrimp are chilled they are excellent with mayonnaise; if warm, just melted butter.

Cooking
Regular Shrimp

Place whole shrimp in a pot and cover shrimp with water or any liquid in which you wish to cook the shrimp. Place lid on slightly askew. Turn burner to high. When steam is puffing out around the top, which is ajar, turn off heat, clamp lid down tight and then drain the water by opening lid "ever so slightly," into the sink.

Next close lid tightly, set pot off burner and let shrimp "steam" for 10 to 15 minutes. Don't peek under lid, for this lets out steam.

Cooking
Rock Shrimp

To boil, place 1½ pounds of rock shrimp in 1 quart of water to which 2 tablespoons of salt have been added and brought to a simmer. Simmer shrimp for 30 to 45 seconds, then rinse in cold water.

To broil, cut shrimp through bottom side where swimmerettes are and all the way to the hard top shell and then spread open. Spread butter or margarine on them and broil about four inches from heat for about 2 minutes or until tails turn upward.

Green Goddess Shrimp Salad

1 pound cooked, peeled, deveined Pacific shrimp or other small shrimp, fresh or frozen

1¼ cups mayonnaise or salad dressing

1 can (2 ounces) or 2 tablespoons anchovy fillets, drained and chopped

2 tablespoons chopped parsley

2 tablespoons chopped chives or green onions and tops

2 tablespoons tarragon vinegar

1 small clove minced garlic

About 3 quarts romaine lettuce, crisped, torn into bite-size pieces

Thaw shrimp if frozen. Combine mayonnaise, anchovy, parsley, chives, vinegar, and garlic; blend flavors for several hours. Makes about 1½ cups dressing. Toss half the dressing (¾ cup) with romaine.

Place about 2 cups of salad mixture on each of six salad plates; portion shrimp equally on top of salads. Spoon remaining salad dressing over shrimp if desired.

Makes 6 servings.

Note: Dressing keeps well in refrigerator for later use.

Stuffed Shrimp

2 pounds raw jumbo shrimp (24 to 30), fresh or frozen
1 can (6½ or 7 ounces) crabmeat, drained, flaked, and
cartilage removed
¼ teaspoon salt
2 teaspoons margarine or butter
¼ cup finely chopped onion
2 tablespoons finely chopped green onion
2 tablespoons finely chopped celery
2 tablespoons finely chopped green pepper
1 tablespoon chopped parsley
1 clove garlic, minced
½ teaspoon salt
¼ teaspoon cayenne pepper
2 eggs, beaten
1 can (5-⅓ ounces) evaporated milk
1 cup all-purpose flour
3 cups soft white bread crumbs
Fat for deep frying

Thaw shrimp if frozen. Shell shrimp, leaving last section of shell and tail intact. Devein, rinse, and drain dry on absorbent paper. Butterfly the shrimp by cutting along their outside curve about three quarters of the way through and carefully flattening them. Sprinkle with salt.

In small saucepan, melt margarine. Add onion, green onion, celery, green pepper, parsley, and garlic. Cover and cook 5 minutes or until tender. Remove from heat. Stir in crabmeat, ½ teaspoon salt, and cayenne. Pack stuffing mixture in a band down the center of each shrimp, dividing it equally among them. Combine eggs and evaporated milk in a shallow bowl.

Place flour and bread crumbs in separate pie plates. One at a time, roll the shrimp in the flour to coat evenly, dip into egg mixture, then roll in bread crumbs. Arrange shrimp on baking sheet and refrigerate one hour to firm coating.

Arrange 5 or 6 shrimp in a single layer in a fry basket. Fry in deep fat, 350° F., for 3 to 5 minutes or until shrimp are brown and done. Drain on absorbent paper. Keep warm in very low oven while remaining shrimp are being cooked.

Makes 6 servings.

Etouffee is a method of cooking something smothered in a blanket of chopped vegetables, over a low flame, in a tightly covered vessel—popular in Louisiana Cajun country for preparing crawfish or shrimp. The exact recipe depends on the cook. As a local proverb has it, "each cook knows his own pot best."

Shrimp Etouffee

3 pounds raw rock shrimp or other shrimp, fresh or frozen
¼ cup margarine or butter
3 tablespoons all-purpose flour
1 cup chopped onion
½ cup chopped celery
¼ cup chopped green pepper
2 tablespoons chopped green onion
2 tablespoons chopped parsley
1 clove garlic, minced
½ cup water
1 tablespoon lemon juice
¼ teaspoon salt
¼ teaspoon cayenne pepper
3 cups cooked rice

Thaw shrimp if frozen. Peel, clean, and rinse shrimp. In 10-inch fry pan melt margarine; blend in flour. Add onion, celery, green pepper, green onion, parsley, and garlic. Cover and cook 5 minutes or until tender. Gradually add water. Stir in lemon juice, salt, and pepper. Push vegetables to one side of pan. Add shrimp to pan; spoon vegetables over shrimp. Cover and simmer for approximately 5 minutes or until shrimp are pink and tender. Serve over rice.

Makes 6 servings.

Carolina Shrimp Pilau

2 pounds raw, peeled, and deveined shrimp, fresh or frozen
8 slices bacon
2 cups chopped onion
1½ cups uncooked long grain rice
3 cups chicken broth or bouillon
1 can (28 ounces) tomatoes, undrained, cut up
2 teaspoons Worcestershire sauce
1 teaspoon salt
1 teaspoon ground mace
¼ teaspoon cayenne pepper
2 tablespoons chopped parsley

Thaw shrimp if frozen. In a heavy 3 to 4 quart Dutch oven cook bacon until crisp. Remove bacon. Drain on absorbent paper. Crumble and set aside. Reserve 3 tablespoons bacon fat.

Add onion to reserved bacon fat. Cover and cook until tender. Stir in rice.

Add chicken broth, tomatoes, Worcestershire sauce, salt, mace, and pepper. Bring to a boil. Cover and bake in a moderate oven 350° F., for 15 minutes.

Stir in shrimp and bacon. Cover and return to oven for 10 minutes or until shrimp are done. Remove from oven, fluff with a fork, and sprinkle with parsley.

Makes 6 servings.

Brandied Rock Shrimp

Because rock shrimp—which were once discarded as unsaleable by fishermen—are a recent arrival to the public, the field is wide open for recipes. Whereas some people consider oysters as over-reciped, there are very few recipes for rock shrimp. Here's one recipe which may break the ground.

1 cup rock shrimp, shelled and deveined
½ stick butter
3 tablespoons brandy
4 slices toast

Cut shrimp into approximately ½-inch pieces. Heat butter and brandy over medium heat until it is light brown (about 5 minutes). Add shrimp and stir for one minute. Place shrimp on toast and pour sauce over them. Serves 2.

Whiskeyed Shrimp

1 lb. jumbo shrimp
3 tablespoons peanut or other oil
1 clove garlic, chopped
4 tablespoons whiskey
4 tablespoons soy sauce
½ cup chicken stock
4 tablespoons chopped onion
Rice (for 4 servings)

Cut shrimp in half lengthwise and devein, but leave shrimp in shells (butterfly). The larger the shrimp, the easier it is to remove the meat from their shells after cooking.

Pour oil in frying pan over medium heat, add shrimp and cook with shells down for 5 minutes. Shake pan often to spread oil. Add garlic, whiskey, soy sauce, chicken stock, and onion. Cover and simmer for 10 to 12 minutes.

Serve shrimp and broth over boiled rice.

Blue Mussel

Striated Mussel

Mussels

Blue mussels, which are almost impossible to buy but can be readily picked from jetties and wrecks, have been described as the perfect food. The only thing you can do wrong with them is not clean them properly. Scrub well and scrape off any barnacles, for they hold sand. Next tear off beard and discard any partially opened mussels or any that float.

Mussels have not been appreciated in America and one reason might be because they are frequently mistaken with striated mussels, shown to the left. These mussels—which even starfish pass over—are muddish brown, ribbed and are found along marshes and in the mud. They help hold the marsh land together, but as a food they are too strong in taste.

Blue mussels, which are shiny, blue-black and smooth are sometimes washed up after storms. There have been some recent attempts to grow them for commercial use. The country would be nutritiously wealthier if they are successful.

Mussel Soup

1 tablespoon onions
½ teaspoon minced garlic
½ cup butter
1 teaspoon parsley
pinch of thyme
½ cup white wine
1 quart mussels

Saute onions, and garlic in 2 tablespoons butter. Add parsley, thyme and wine.

Simmer for 5 minutes.

Add mussels and cook until open.

Scallops

You can easily buy scallop meat and you can easily buy scallop shells, but rarely can you buy scallop meat in their shells. If you could, you would probably eat more of the scallop than the "eye," really the adductor muscle. North Americans have the dubious distinction of being the only people who don't eat all of the scallop meat.

One reason you normally can't buy scallops in their shells, is because scallops can't keep their mouths shut, often chattering and clattering like castanets after being brought aboard. Unable to maintain their life saving juices, the scallops expire. The scallop boats stay out at sea for weeks so the shuckers find it more expedient to save and refrigerate the eye and feed the rest to the little fish.

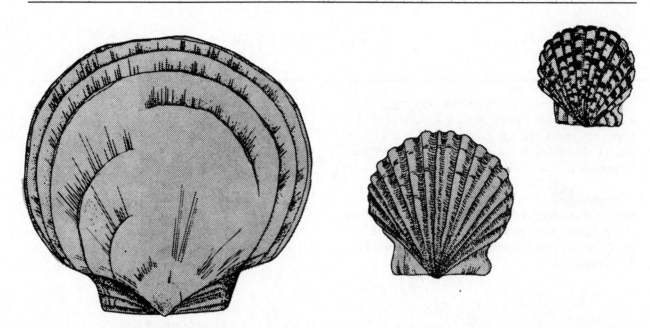

The scallops above were drawn by Jane Law for *Coastwatch*, published by The University of North Carolina. From left to right are Ocean Scallops, Bay Scallops and Calico Scallops. They have been drawn at about half their adult size.

There are several directions for opening scallops which range from simply placing a sharp blade between the shells and cutting the adductor muscle to placing the scallops on a warm stove until they start to open and then cutting out the eye or the muscle.

Then there is this thorough description on how to open scallops from *Making a Living Alongshore*, by Phil Schwind. After giving explicit instructions on how to tape your hands in preparation for opening scallops, he directs.

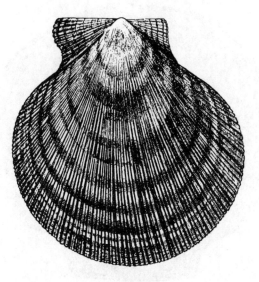

Pecten islandicus

If the scallop is equally clean on both sides, as sometimes happens with scallops living in clear sand, make sure the straight edge of the scallop is to your right, the indented side to your left.

"Put the padded ball of your right thumb on the top shell, holding the knife between the tips of your fingers and the palm of the same hand. Bring the knife point to the opening between the shells, just where the straight edge swells to the shell proper. Insert the point and slightly twist the edge up and the back down. If the scallop shells are brittle, this twist should be very light, or it will break a corner off the top shell. By twisting the knife slightly and sliding the point pressed against the top shell halfway through the scallop, you should be able to cut the adductor muscle clear of the top shell. A slight flipping motion away from you should lift the top shell clear. Now slide the knife point in against the bottom shell, under the guts, at about "two o'clock" (reading the scallop as a clock, with 11 o'clock at the top away from you). Slide the knife point counterclockwise around the adductor muscle, from two to 10 o'clock. As the point reaches 10 o'clock . . .

. . . lift and flip the gut toward you, squeezing the edge of the gut lightly between your right thumb and the knife blade . . . then scrape the adductor muscle off the shell with the knife blade, scraping toward and using your right thumb as a kind of stop. A flick of your right wrist will pop the scallop—or the part you want—into the stainless pan. Before it lands, you should have dropped shell and guts into the barrel between your legs, and your left hand should be reaching for another scallop."

Cooking Scallops

Scallops should never be cooked and then re-warmed. They have to be cooked once and quickly. Of course, they are delicious raw.

Galloping Scallops

The following is hardly a recipe. Place scallops on a red hot skillet and cauterize them. The scallops will dance and sizzle, but a lot of this is because they have been soaked in water after they were shucked and this makes them swell and, of course, weigh and cost more.

Sear scallops until they are light brown and then serve with melted butter and lemon or mayonnaise.

Scallops and Turnips

1 cup diced scallops
1 cup diced turnips
1 cup chopped spinach
Mix the above
1 tablespoon sherry or vermouth
1 tablespoon butter

Heat the butter and sherry over medium heat. Add the mixture of scallops, turnips and spinach and stir for one minute.

Point Judith Scallops

1 pound scallops, fresh or frozen
¼ cup margarine or butter
1 cup sliced fresh mushrooms
¼ cup margarine or butter
2 tablespoons minced onion
2 tablespoons all-purpose flour
½ teaspoon salt
1½ cups half and half
4 egg yolks, beaten
½ teaspoon leaf thyme
¼ teaspoon basil leaves
½ cup fresh bread crumbs
⅓ cup grated Swiss Gruyere cheese
¼ teaspoon paprika
1 tablespoon melted margarine or butter

Thaw scallops if frozen. Remove any shell particles and wash. In a skillet melt margarine. Add
scallops and mushrooms. Cook for 3 to 4 minutes or
until scallops are done. Divide scallops and
mushrooms into 6 individual shells or ramekins. In a
small saucepan melt ¼ cup margarine. Add onion and
cook until tender. Stir in flour and salt. Gradually stir
in half and half. Cook until thickened, stirring
constantly.

Add a little of the hot sauce to the egg yolks; add
to remaining sauce, stirring constantly. Heat just until thickened. Stir in thyme and basil. Spoon sauce over
scallops. Combine bread crumbs, cheese, paprika, and
margarine. Sprinkle on top of sauce. Place shells on
a baking tray and bake in a hot oven, 400° F., for 10
to 15 minutes or until hot and bubbly.

Makes 6 servings.

Remoulade Sauce

A classic French sauce based on a blend of mustard, oil, vinegar, and seasonings. New Orleans Remoulade Sauce is served cold. Highly seasoned and reddish in color, it is spooned over shrimp, crab, or scallops and served as an appetizer, but can double as a main dish salad when served in an avocado half. It is considered one of the best Creole recipes New Orleans has to offer.

¼ cup tarragon vinegar
2 tablespoons prepared brown mustard
1 tablespoon catsup
1½ teaspoons paprika
½ teaspoon salt
¼ teaspoon cayenne pepper
½ cup salad oil
¼ cup chopped celery
¼ cup chopped green onion
1 tablespoon chopped parsley

In small bowl combine vinegar, mustard, catsup, paprika, salt, and cayenne. Slowly add salad oil, beating constantly. (May also be done in a blender.)

Stir in celery, green onion, and parsley. Allow to stand 3 or 4 hours to blend flavors.

Makes 1¼ cups sauce.

Scallop Remoulade Appetizer

1½ pounds bay scallops or other scallops, fresh or frozen
1 cup water
½ cup dry white wine
2 slices onion
2 sprigs parsley
½ teaspoon salt
¼ teaspoon thyme
Shredded lettuce
Remoulade Sauce
Hard cooked egg, optional

Thaw scallops if frozen. Remove any remaining pieces of shell. Rinse with cold water and drain. In saucepan combine water, wine, onion, parsley, salt, and thyme; bring to a boil. Place scallops in poaching liquid; cover and simmer 2 to 5 minutes or until tender. Drain scallops and chill.

Arrange scallops on a bed of shredded lettuce in individual seafood shells or in cocktail glasses. Spoon about 3½ tablespoons Remoulade sauce on top of each serving. Garnish with chopped hard cooked egg, if desired.

Makes 6 servings.

Whelks

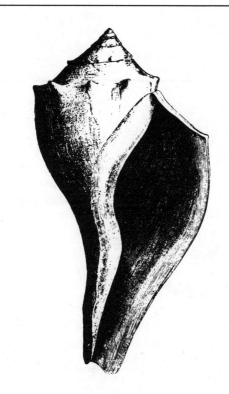

Channeled and knobbed whelks, often called conchs, abound in the bays and ocean in the Mid Atlantic areas, living mostly off hard shell clams, which is reason enough to eat them more often.

There is a method of getting the animal out of the shell by punching a hole in the second spiral from the outside and then cutting the muscle holding the animal inside free. This takes practice and many of the whelks you pick up will be too small to do this.

Another very expedient way is to smash the shell with a hammer and pick out the meat and wash off the broken shell. However, if (and excuse the pun) you would like to have your conch and eat it too, boil it for 10 or 15 minutes until you can pull the animal free. The undamaged shell can be used for an ornament.

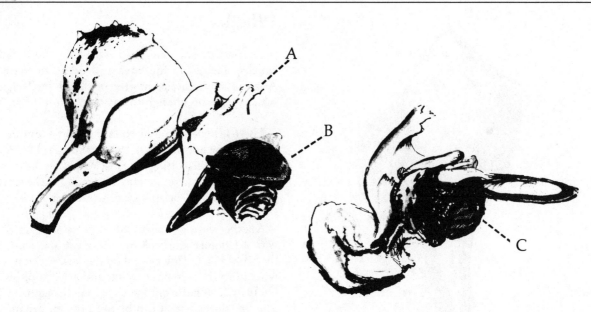

Shown is the whole animal extracted from its shell. Discard the orange viscera (A) and the horney black operculum (B), which is like a trap door. The meat is inside a gray black knob.

The foot, (C) which is black in color on the outside, but the color of chicken breast inside is what you want to eat eventually. It has the texture of rubber and it's one of the few foods you'll find that bounces.

Carve into very thin slices, discarding any part that isn't white.

Whelk Chowder

Once you have the slices, pound them with a mallet or the edge of a plate to break down their toughness. You can marinate the slices in lime juice for several hours, or use meat tenderizer.

Once the meat is broken down, it's ready to be cooked any way other shellfish is cooked, but it's best in stews.

Most seafood is more attractive than the animal inside a conch or whelk—and it does make you wonder how the shell can be so beautiful, yet its occupant so hideously ugly. However, they are tasty.

6 whelks or conchs
1 sweet pepper (seeded)
1 clove garlic
1 carrot
2 large onions (peeled)
1 stalk celery
Butter, fat or oil (approximately 3 tablespoons)
Thyme, salt and pepper
1 28-oz. can of tomatoes
two-thirds cup tomato paste
2 cups of stock, preferably fish stock
1 cup broken up saltines or dry biscuits
3 cups sherry

Put whelks and vegetables through a meat grinder.

Saute mixture in butter for 10 minutes.

Add seasonings, tomatoes, paste, and stock and cook 10 minutes.

Mix in saltines, and simmer for one hour.

Add sherry just before serving.

Note that any seafood from chunks of fish to any shellfish can be added to the whelk or replace it. Also the chowder can be thickened by adding flour and butter. Serves 6.

Cioppino

¼ cup peanut oil or any kind of oil
1 clove garlic minced
1 onion chopped
2 cups canned tomatoes
½ cup wine
Clams
Shrimp
Lobster tails
Mussels
King Crab legs
Flounder filets

Saute onions and garlic in oil. Add tomatoes and wine and simmer until blended. Add all seafood except shrimp to sauce and simmer until shellfish and fish are cooked. Clams should open. Add shrimp after clams open and simmer until shrimp turns pink.

The above recipe can also become "Mussels Marinara" by adding only mussels to the sauce, steaming them until the mussels open and serving over a bed of freshly cooked linguini or white rice.

Squid

Of all shellfish, and fin fish, too, for that matter, squid supplies a more edible portion of its body; up to 80 percent. Besides that, it is one of the cheapest of seafood for it is also used for bait.

Cut off tentacles and arms just in front of eyes.

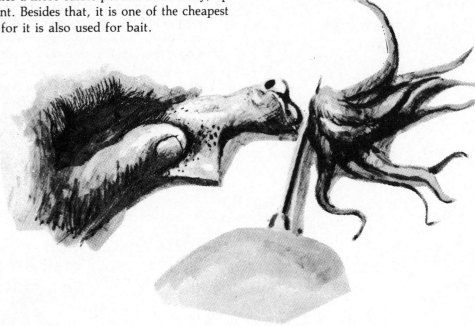

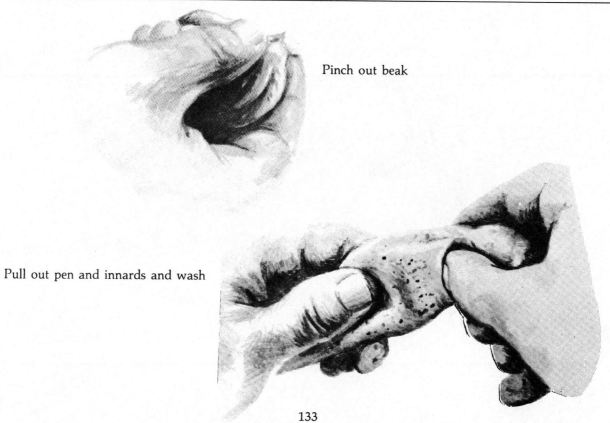

Pinch out beak

Pull out pen and innards and wash

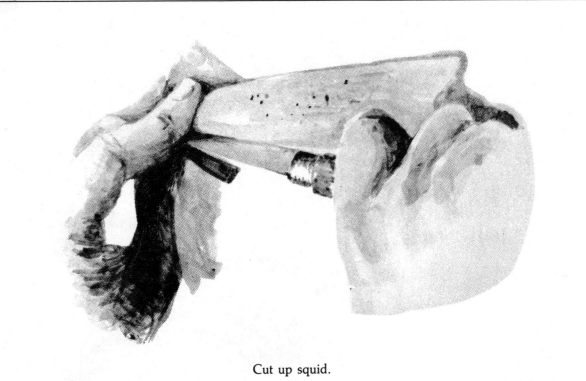

Cut up squid.

The California squid fishery began in Monterey Bay about 1863, when a Chinese fishing village was established near Mussel Point. Chinese and Japanese fishermen rowed a skiff with a blazing torch around the Bay until a school of squid was attracted to it. Two accompanying skiffs would than set a small purse seine.

Traditionally popular with Americans of Oriental or Mediterranean ancestry, squid are increasing in popularity in many areas. To broaden the appeal of the following dish, the recipe uses familiar American ingredients.

In 1905, Italian fishermen introduced the lampara net to Monterey Bay, and significantly improved the efficiency of the California squid fishery. The Mediterranean influence is reflected in the recipe on page 137: *calamari* is Italian for squid and the French term *vinaigrette* is substituted for the less familiar Italian *olie e aceto*, oil and vinegar.

Stuffed Squid Monterey

2 pounds whole squid, fresh or frozen
1 cup chopped onion
⅔ cup chopped carrot
½ cup melted margarine or butter
4 cups fresh bread crumbs
⅔ cup chopped parsley
4 teaspoons dry sherry
¼ teaspoon salt
⅛ teaspoon pepper
Margarine or butter for frying

Thaw squid if frozen. Cut through arms near the eyes. With the thumb and forefinger, squeeze out the inedible beak which will be located near the cut. Chop tentacles and reserve for stuffing. Feel inside the mantle for chitinous pen. Firmly grasp pen and attached viscera; remove from mantle. Wash mantle thoroughly and drain.

Cook onion, carrot, and chopped tentacles in melted margarine until tender. Stir in crumbs, parsley, sherry, salt, and pepper. Stuff squid loosely. Close opening with small skewer or toothpick if desired. Fry over moderately high heat in margarine or half margarine and half oil for 3 to 4 minutes; turn carefully and fry 3 to 4 minutes on other side just until squid is cooked.

Makes 6 entree servings or 12 appetizer servings.

Calamari Vinaigrette

2 pounds whole squid, fresh or frozen
2 cups boiling water
2 teaspoons salt
1 lemon
¼ cup olive oil
2 tablespoons vinegar
1½ teaspoons lemon juice
½ teaspoon salt
¼ teaspoon pepper, freshly ground
Salad greens
Chopped parsley

Thaw squid if frozen. Cut through arms near the eyes. With thumb and forefinger, squeeze out the inedible beak which will be located near the cut. Reserve whole tentacles. Remove clear chitinous pen from inside the body mantle. Firmly grasp pen and attached viscera; remove from mantle. Wash mantle thoroughly and drain. Cut mantle crosswise into rings. Remove peel from lemon, combine boiling water, salt, and squid rings and tentacles; simmer for 3 minutes. Add lemon peel and simmer 5 minutes longer or until squid is tender. Drain and rinse in cold water. Drain.

Combine olive oil, vinegar, lemon juice, salt, and pepper. Pour vinaigrette over squid; cover and chill. Drain squid and serve on salad greens. Garnish with chopped parsley. Serve as an appetizer alone or on an antipasto tray.

Makes 6 servings.

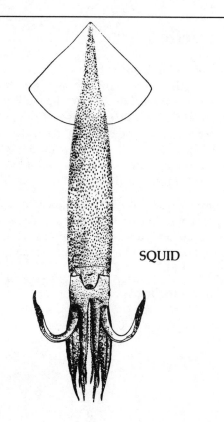

SQUID

Squid Marseillaise

3 pounds whole squid, fresh or frozen
3 tablespoons oil
1½ cups grated carrot
1 cup chopped onion
1 teaspoon salt
1 cup dry white wine
1½ cups water
⅔ cup prunes, quartered

Thaw frozen squid. Clean squid according to procedure 1. Cut squid mantles into eighths. Saute squid in oil. Add carrot and onion and cook few minutes longer. Add salt, wine, and water and cook approximately 40 minutes.

Add prunes and simmer additional 15 minutes or until squid is tender. Serve over rice.

Makes 4 servings.

More implements are used on shellfish than on any other food.

There are dozens of styles of knives manufactured for opening oysters alone. And many shuckers make their own knives, adding still more to the variety. The lowly clam has been the incentive for diversified devices, including a guillotine-type apparatus for separating its shells. The Cadillac of shellfish, the lobster, requires the same instruments you would use to open nuts, but it too has generated a new type instrument that resembles a can opener to slit the shell. Shrimp, one of the easiest shellfish to open, has driven inventors to come up with various ramming instruments. The crab with its intricate and labyrinthic inner structure is often the victim of a demolishing whack from a mallet. Still, it is the subject and source for a range of implements, including a saw-like knife and a pick that would make a dentist's hands itch to hold. The conch and whelk require a hammer, knife and pliers to wrest out the animal inside, whereas a pin is all that is needed to pick out the meat from a periwinkle.

The above listing only touches on the varieties of devices used by individuals. It does not include the machine used to remove meat in large quantities and apparently now even laser beams are being tested for opening oysters.

Unless you go to a raw bar or a restaurant, you are usually left to your own devices to open shellfish. Fortunately, there are many devices from which to chose.

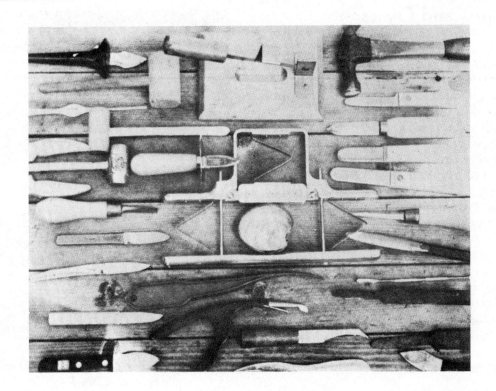

For Clams and Oysters:

Perhaps the best method of opening a clam is by sliding a thin and narrow blade like those on a vegetable or fillet knife in the soft spot where the hinge of the clam is located. Once inside, work the blade sideways so that it severs both adductor muscles. You should not have to force the blade. If you do, then you haven't penetrated the clam properly. Try again. Once the muscles are cut, the clam releases its grip and then you can go into the front of the clam and scoop out the meat.

One method which is easier still and requires the use of a file or rough area such as cement is to scrape the edge of the clam until you have a small opening and then enter with a knife. Just be careful not to let any of the powder in.

In opening shellfish, you should never have part of your body in the course of the implement. If it slips, the injury could be severe.

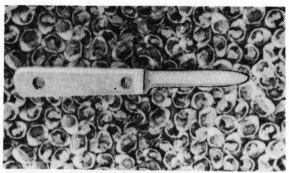

Standard Clam Knife For Small Clams

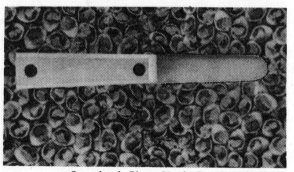

Standard Clam Knife For Large Clams

The grill brush is great for cleaning clams, oysters, mussels, and, of course, grills. Be careful of the bristles because they are sharp. Remember to wear gloves.

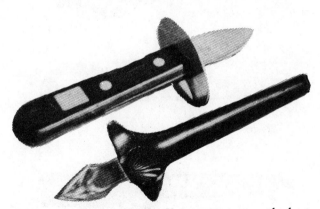

These two German Oyster Knives are among the best made.

The cleanest method of opening an oyster is by popping it open. You work a strong blade into the pointed end where the hinge is located. By twisting and crowbaring the blade, pry the oyster open. You are ripping the shells from its adductor muscle rather than by cutting the muscle. After the shell is open, you have to go in and cut the meat free. Sometimes, with an extremely large and obstinate oyster, you must drive the blade in by hammering the other end with a heavy object.

The knives to use for this method are the short-bladed foreign knives or a Gulf or Southern knife. Also, the Carvel Hall Crack knife is an excellent tool for opening oysters in this fashion.

Remember, you need a strong blade and strong wrist. See pages 79 to 84.

The Carvel Hall Breaker (Crack knife)

Oyster knives will vary in size and shape depending upon the type and size of the oyster, the shucking method being used and, most importantly, the personal preference of the user.

The New Haven (Murphy)
2½" Bent Tip Blade

A French-made Oyster Knife with Hilt by Rowoco

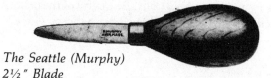

The Seattle (Murphy)
2½" Blade

These are but a few of the Oyster Knives available. For further information on these and other devices, check page 153.

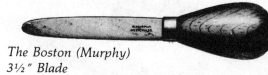

The Boston (Murphy)
3½" Blade

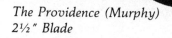

The Providence (Murphy)
2½" Blade

For Crabs:

The knife should have a sharp point to get every bit of crab possible.

Above is the professional crab knife. Often law requires that it must be made of one piece of metal so that bits of crab cannot be stuck in crevices for bacteria to flourish. Also, the professional crab knife usually has a rounded and not a sharp blade so that professional pickers cannot nick or stab themselves.

One of the more interesting crab knives created by the late Mr. Thomas Kneavel, who made a little saw with a sharp screwdriver-shaped blade. He would cut out the underside of the crab and then use the sharp blade to push down and cut the crab shell. It is an effective instrument.

All Metal Mallet

Wooden Mallet

Mallet With Metal Handle And Wooden Head

145

For Shrimp and Lobster:

Among the many implements used to clean shrimp, the device above is especially useful. One push along the shrimp's backside does it.

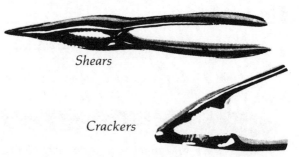

Shears

Crackers

Lobster shears and nut crackers are useful household items—especially for lobster.

Pictured above is a shell slitter, which can be used for lobster and rock shrimp shells.

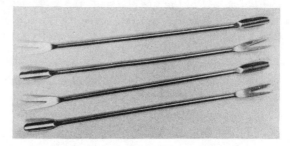

Picks can make eating lobster and crabs much easier.

Rather than purchasing crabs at a local fishmarket or roadside stand, an enjoyable and inexpensive way to obtain the shellfish needed for a sumptuous feast is to spend a day crabbing. This is a sport that is easy to learn and also provides a great deal of pleasure and excitement—as well as some excellent eating.

The most common method for catching crabs is the use of hand lines and scoop nets. This method can be used as long as the water is clear, calm, and relatively shallow, and the weather is cooperative. All you really need is some good, strong cord, a weight (about 3 to 4 ounces) for each line you want to place, some bait, and a scoop net. Begin by cutting a piece of cord long enough to reach from the object you wish to secure it to (dock, a permanent object on the shore, a stake driven into the floor of the body of water, or the side of the boat) to the bottom of the water, with room to spare. Tie on the weight about a foot from one end of the cord, then tie on the bait near or over the weight. Cut off the dangling end of the cord. Secure the other end of the line to the object you have chosen, then carefully drop the weight into the water. When choosing the object to which the line will be secured, be sure that you will be able to reach the water with your scoop net from that point. A long handle net will give you more flexibility in the number of sites you can use for this crabbing method, but will take more practice to control.

After waiting a few minutes from the time the lines were dropped into the water, lightly pick up the line with your thumb and forefinger to determine if a crab is on the line. If so, *gently* ease up on the line, inch by inch, so that the crab is unaware that he is being lifted from the bottom. When you can see the crab near the surface, hold the line with one hand and quickly scoop down alongside and under the crab, and then scoop up by turning your wrist. The crab, line, bait, and weight should be in your net. The crab should then be placed in a proper receptacle by turning the net over. As it is vital that the crab be kept alive until cooking time, a bushel basket or burlap sack that allows breathing are recommended.

If the weather and water conditions are not ideal, or you don't have the patience or dexterity for handlines, you may want to use either traps or pots, as most commercial crabbers now employ. The difference between a trap and a pot is simple. If the crab can enter and leave the equipment at any time before

147

a physical act by the crabber, it is a trap. If the crab cannot exit once it enters, the gear is a pot.

No matter which of the three types of traps you use, square, pyramid, or open end wire basket, make sure that the bait is tied tightly inside the trap and that there is sufficient cord to allow the trap to rest on the bottom of the water. The side panels will open and also lie flat on the bottom, allowing the crab easy entrance to the bait. Wait a few minutes after dropping the trap and pull up quickly, holding the line tightly. This pulls up the side panels and traps any crabs which may be inside the trap. Take the trap to the receptacle, open one panel, and allow the crabs to drop into it. This procedure can be repeated until the receptacle is full.

The crab pot, which can be purchased for about $20, is a much larger and heavier piece of equipment, weighing up to fifteen pounds when baited and weighted. The pot is generally only brought to the surface a few times a day, but requires strength, as a pot full of crabs may weigh forty pounds or more. The two types of crab pots are the Maryland crab pot (cubicle in structure) and the round wire pot, used on the West Coast. Once the pot is baited and lowered into the water, a floating buoy, marked according to the particular state law (by color, name, or number) must be attached to the other end of the rope. Once a crab enters the pot, it is not likely to escape. The main reason that the pot must be retrieved at least once a day is to insure that the crabs are alive when they reach the surface.

No matter which method of crabbing you use, it is important that you are familiar with your individual state laws to determine which methods are acceptable, what sizes of crabs you may keep, and the maximum number of crabs you may catch. Again, when the catch is safely home, only cook and eat those crabs that are alive and kicking until dropped in the pot.

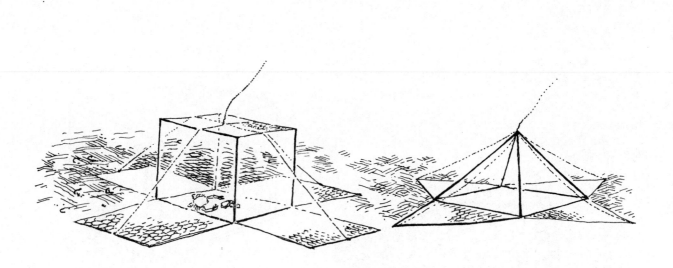

*The Square and Pyramid Wire Traps lie flat on the
bottom but close when they are pulled to the surface.*

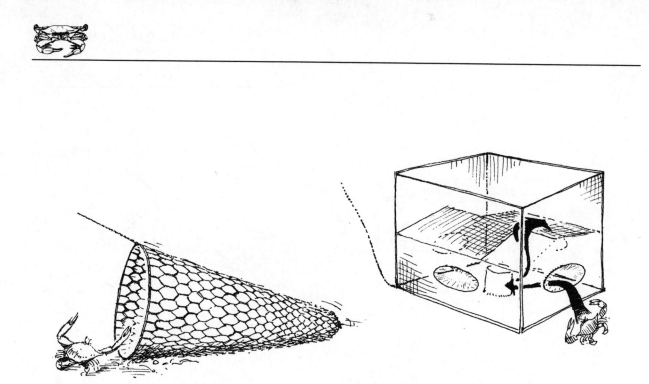

The Open End Wire Basket will catch crabs if it is pulled to the surface quickly.

A crab enters one of the four side openings in the Maryland Crab Pot, eats the bait, and tends to rise through the two openings (above) to the second level and becomes trapped.

Acknowledgements and Credits

The author and publisher thank the following people: Daniel G. Coston, Jr. for his illustrations; Theodore Reinke for his expertise as technical advisor; and Colleen Palmer Ballant for her editorial assistance and recipe for Creamy Crab Chowder.

Suppliers of Shellfish Knives and Other Devices

Rowoco, Inc.
Building 4, Warehouse Lane
Elmsford, NY 10523

Carvel Hall
Crisfield, MD 21817

R. Murphy, Inc.
13 Groton-Harvard Road
P.O. Box 376
Ayer, MA 01432

Titles in the Shellfish Series

The Craft of Dismantling Crabs
The Shellfish Heritage Cookbook
Left To Your Own Devices
The Illustrious Oyster Illustrated
Clambake Sans Sand In Pots and Woks

For ordering or additional information, write to:

Shellfish Series
P.O. Box 469
Georgetown, DE 19947